KORALY DIMITRIADIS

First published in 2024
Outside The Box Press
www.outsidetheboxpress.com

Copyright © Koraly Dimitriadis 2024

The moral right of the author has been asserted.

All rights reserved.
No part of this publication may be reproduced or transmitted by any person or entity (including Google, Amazon or similar organisations), in any form or means, electronic or mechanical, including photocopying, recording, scanning or by any information storage and retrieval system without prior permission in writing
from the author.

ISBN 978-0-6457752-0-4

Cover design by Rosie G

Author photograph by Kaliopi Malamas

Design and typesetting by Outside The Box Press
www.outsidetheboxpress.com

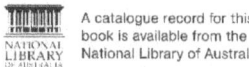
A catalogue record for this book is available from the National Library of Australia

Praise for Koraly Dimitriadis

"Relentlessly bold, unapologetic, and humorous at all the right times. If one can detect a new wave of Australian poetry on the rise, it's due in no small part to the pioneering efforts of Koraly Dimitriadis."
– Ruby Hamad, author, *White Tears, Brown Scars*

"Ms Dimitriadis is the voice of an angry Australia. Her anger is for the disaffected, the voiceless and the invisible.
– Paul Capsis, award-winning performer

"She dishes the dirt, and she's not afraid of anything. Her writing is coming for you, so you'd better just accept it ... a voice that literally demands to be heard."
– *Overland Literary Journal*

"The kind of honesty that can only come about after being wound-up, held writhing, repressed and silenced."
– *Disclaimer Magazine (UK)*

"She is merciless ... astounding." **– Stage Whispers**

"... a voice of reason or a reckless rebel."
– Channel Nine News

"A traditionalist's nightmare ... searingly honest explorations of life ..." **– *Junkee***

"Dimitriadis' poems are explosively political and humane."
– Andy Jackson, award-winning poet, *Human Looking*

Also by Koraly Dimitriadis

Love and Fuck Poems
Just Give Me The Pills
The Mother Must Die (2024)

For Ania Walwicz

Contents

Preface 1

She's not normal 2

The Box 4

The Great Australian Dream 16

The Literary Judge 32

A Fucking Arsehole-Of-A-Man Killed His Wife 48

Thin 84

Romantic 105

Who is she? 133

Cutting Through The Bullshit 156

Credits 185

Acknowledgments 187

About The Author 188

Index 190

Preface

The following poems span 12 years of life. They are not in chronological order. Occasionally I provided a date, if context is required. The most recent poem, 'I write my poems on the fly', was written in early 2021, but many of my poems, from 2021 and prior, are still unpublished. The poems in this book helped me move through and into the next chapter of my life. I feel I have outgrown some of them, but still want to share to perhaps inspire others.

I wanted to play around with the word 'normal' with this book, not only with my views and poetic form, but also with the structure of the collection, and the way in which I have birthed the book into the world. Despite being a bestselling poet in Australia (as confirmed by bookshops including Readings), I still have not been able to secure a publisher for my poetry. My short story collection is forthcoming with Puncher and Wattmann, and this will be my first publication with an Australian publisher, but my poetry is still constantly rejected. So I decided at the last minute, after receiving funding from the Cypriot government, to launch in Cyprus ONLY, with the rest of the world, including Australia, to wait until I'm ready. I did this in an attempt to break free from the shackles of the publishing world, which constantly tells me my writing is not good enough.

Notes: The term 'wog' has its own unique context in Australia. A racial slur against Mediterranean migrants, it was reclaimed in the 90s with highly successful and acclaimed 'wog comedy'. Themes of suicide and violence against women are present in this book. When I separated from my husband in 2010 I knew nothing of feminism. I was married at age 22.

She's not normal

Why isn't she normal?
Why can't she be normal?
Why can't she say normal things?
She's not normal
Why can't she be normal?
She makes me feel really uncomfortable
I caaaaaan't…
Because she's not normal
Why can't she be normal?
And do normal things
And speak in normal ways
And say normal things
And do normal things
Just be normal
Go-o-o-o-o-d, it's just, it's just so infuriating
It makes me cringe
It makes me feel…shit
Whyyyyyy? Why can't she be normal?
Why can't she be like us?
Why can't she be like everyone else?
Why? What's wrong with her?
There's nothing wrong me
There's something wrong with her
And her friends
And people like her
What's wrong with them?
Why can't they just be like us?
Like just normal
It's weird
It must be her parents
Or something, something went wrong

Something happened
And now she's just not normal
I wish she was
She makes me feel terrible
Go-o-o-od, I hope she finds the help she needs
I hope she gets what she needs
& finds what she needs, I really do
I really hope, I really pray,
that she does get the help that she needs
So she can just be normal
And then I won't have to feel like this
Why can't her life be normal?
Like the things that she does, in her life?
Why can't they be normal?
Why? I don't understand
There's a way things should be done
What's wrong with her?
Why is she like that? I don't get it

The Box

The world
(2009)

I was asked to write a poem
on how I perceive the world.

At first I thought it was a joke.
I laughed so hard my tummy hurt.
The world's good like that –
it cracks you up sometimes.

My laughter was out of control:
tears were sliding down my face,
I was clutching my stomach,
and people were looking at me funny
like 'why is she laughing like that?'
and I tell you, I felt like peeing,
right there on the spot.
I was laughing so hard
I wasn't even sure if
I was actually laughing
or crying, because then I was
really crying and then laughing
but it was more like crying
or was it laughing, and
it was hard to tell
which one
it was.

It must be a joke.

Because on some days
the world invites me to relish
in lush greens and picnics baskets

sweet strawberries and frolicking

and on others, it pollutes my soul,
and all I want to do is stay home
immerse myself in a bath of steamy water

to slash my wrists.

This poem is a joke.

You want to know what the world sounds like?
It sounds like the same song repeated
over and over and over again,
broken records, stacked to the heavens
like corporate buildings.

No wonder they want to blow them up.

Me? My world is a glasshouse,
one I shrill in like mute storms
to explode like a slow-mo film

see   me   reflected   in

    shards   of   glass

falling   poetically   to   me

        Quick

        Duck.

The world is narrow
one-tenth shown
one-tenth experienced
one-tenth enjoyed.
The rest is draped
in black curtains of
newspapers and
television.

Come close –
the truths of the world
are spoken in whispers:

The world is a drone.
The world smells decayed.
It tastes, like rivers of blood
It feels like razors
It sounds like
a car accident.

This is no joke.

I am angry because
(2015)

I am angry because
I'm thirty-something years old
I am angry because
I'm a single parent
I am angry because
my princess doesn't wake with me
50% of the time
& says she misses me
even when she's
in my presence

I am angry because
I cried all the time when I was little
Angry because I only just realised
that all the people picking on me
at primary school were Aussie boys
& wog boys and wog girls
(everyone, basically)

I'm angry because my dad
grew up in a remote village in Cyprus
& came to Australia for a better life
only to have his daughter angry that
she didn't get to grow up in Cyprus

I'm angry because I don't belong here
I'm angry because I don't belong here
I'm angry because I don't belong anywhere
I'm angry because I'm sad
I'm sad. I'm so sad.

The world's interests

Why is the world
more interested
in seeing someone being shot
than a woman's vagina?
Why is it okay
with seeing a building blown up,
millions of people massacred,
a child being bashed
rather than a man's penis?
Or a man's cum?
Why does the world think it appropriate
to depict violence in movies & films & books,
to promote these things to our children,
but not appropriate
to depict graphic sex?
Is the human body
in all its glory
that terrible?
that wrong?
that we are willing to erase it with a

stabbing?

slaughter the body
rather than celebrate it?
hide the body
kill the body
rather than display it?
What would the world be like
if all the violent images
were replaced with sexual ones?
What would the human race evolve to?

Sure, we'd probably have more sex
More enjoyable sex
Less shameful sex
Less underground sex
Less rape?
Less murder?
Would the world be kinder?
Prettier?
Wiser?
Sure, they'd be more babies
But would there be less war?
Less famine?
Less manipulation?
More love?
Is loving the body that bad?

The box

Someone said, stay in the box
Don't make us sad
Stay in the box
I wanted to write a symphony
They said stay in the box
I wanted to run
They said stay in the box
But I wanted to be brave
I wanted to be wild
I wanted to be free
Instead, I learned how to cook

Don't you feel bad?
Stay in the box
Don't you feel bad?
Stay in the box
Don't you feel bad?
Stay in the box
Stay in the box
Stay in the box

He's going to open it
Stay in the box
He took me out
Stay in the box
I'm out of the box
I'm out of the box
I'm out of the box!

Now I can dance
Now I can speak
Now I am able to be me

I am waltzing with government policy
Feminist rights inserted an IUD in me
I speak my mind and people stop talking to me
But how can this be?
If I'm not in the box?

An IUD impregnates me
But I don't want the baby
Nobody will terminate it for me
The air turns to mud
The trees turn to hay
I try to push through
To get out of here
But that's when I realise:

I'm in another box
I'm in a **bigger** box
I'm still in a box
I'm still in a box

It's a much bigger box but it's still a box
Its walls are reinforced with politically correct glue
I'm screaming and shrilling and making so much noise
Because I'm still in a box
I'm still in a box
I'm STILL IN A BOX!

Don't you feel guilty?
Look at all the noise you've caused
Interrupting the status quo
Look at what you did
Why did you do that?
Shut up!
Stay in the box

Stay in the box
Stay in the box

But I'm getting weak in this box
I can't breathe properly in this box
I feel myself getting sick
I am getting sick
I don't understand
I just want to be me

Don't you feel bad?
Don't you care?
There are others more important than you that need the air
Why are you so angry?
Why are you so aggressive?
Can't you just stay quiet?
Stay in the box
Stay in the box

But I'm going to blow it up
Stay in the box
Stay in the box
Stay in the box

Dumb woman

It's easier to be a dumb woman
than a smart one

It's safer too

To be into makeup and boys
& that's about it

It's better to be clueless

People will like you more for it,
if you act like you don't know what you are doing,
that you need guidance of some kind

You won't feel as estranged
from loved ones and your community
if you refrain from speaking up
when you see injustices
when you see someone has
done something that contributes
to the problem of why we should
be dumb in the first place

You will be embraced and supported

But if you are purported to be anything but
going with the grain of how things should be
then you're going to find it very hard indeed

You won't have any success at all in life

You will be shunned
You will be ignored
You will be snubbed

Until you learn your lesson
And return to conforming
To how things should be done

The Great Australian Dream

The work arsehole monster

Behold, the work arsehole monster
You better watch your back
It's out to get you
& blame you
for shit you didn't do
It's got an agenda,
aims, goals
It doesn't see logic
(only it's own)
It's ready to crush you
for all its inadequacies
Heaven forbid it turns around
& looks itself in the mirror
Behold & beware
The work arsehole monster
It's not an apparition or a nightmare
It comes to life
through your computer screen
It can start off as a male boss
but then it can grow a bitch head
& suddenly two are coming at you
Beware
Work arsehole monster
Watch your back
Work arsehole monster
It doesn't know empathy
All it cares about is greed and money
It's got an agenda and a dagger
& it's ready to stab you in the back
When you least expect it
Beware

Most of Melbourne is depressed

Most of Melbourne is depressed,
and why wouldn't we be?

We only got a handful of beach days
last summer, and the summer before that
& the summer before that
Why do people come here, I don't get it?
Yes, we have a thriving night scene
Art coming out of every one of our pores
But we don't have the essentials
We don't have sunshine
And when it happens to make an appearance
we scrummage for it like it's lost treasure

(Look, I found some sun!
Quick, come outside, quick! Quick!)

People from all over Australia come and live here
People from *Perth*
I say, stay over there in your sunshine
& save yourself
It's so cold and miserable here
you just want to step out onto the street
and have a car flatten you
or something

Most of Melbourne is depressed
because many of us came from somewhere else
My parents were born in Cyprus,
therefore all my DNA is Cypriot
& my body, my brain, it's not meant for this climate

It needs long, extended doses of natural vitamin D
so it gets depressed and doesn't want to extend past
    tomorrow,
my DNA cannot acclimatise to misery and sorrow
It is meant to be enjoying summer 80% of the year

And where Sydney Road Brunswick is
in relation to my house, along that strip
there's meant to be a long stretch of Mediterranean Sea
And I'm meant to be elongating my
bikini wearing body there,
dreaming and believing in fairy-tale love,
because my heart is Cypriot
and Cyprus is the island of Aphrodite
and everyone is in love there

instead of having a virus
which lasts two weeks
and the guy you're seeing
doesn't want a relationship
but he's not the right guy for you
no guy is after your *divorce*
Still, you obsess over everything
because you're a wog and always will be
& you're not meant to be living here
you're meant to be living over there
but it's not as if your problems
will disappear if you live in Cyprus
because to them
you're an Aussie
and always will be
so either way
you're just fucked!

Mediterranean madness

You didn't know what to do
with my Mediterranean madness

When I listen to Greek music
I sing to the undying love
of the Greek mentality

When we were together
I would give it to you,
my Mediterranean gift,
my passionate Mediterranean madness
But you, Aussie blue
didn't know what to do
didn't know where to put it
how to fit it, inside you

Once you joked that you'd throw rocks
at my window if I didn't answer my door
& I responded that one night
when I couldn't sleep
I thought you were throwing rocks
at my window
But then you laughed and said
you'd never do anything like that,
it's not you,
& I said, 'I would
it's all that Mediterranean madness'
But you, Aussie blue
didn't know what to do,
didn't know where to put it
how to fit it, inside you

And now, we're no longer together

I sing to Greek songs in my living room
and I imagine you coming to my house
driven by the drop of Mediterranean madness
you accidentally swallowed through our kiss
I imagine you resting your head against my door
listening to my Greek singing
almost ready to knock…

But you don't, because it's not you
Aussie blue, you don't know what to do
All that passion
And so you leave and wonder
why I'm not knocking at *your* door
where *my* Mediterranean madness has gone to

But I swallowed some too, baby
I swallowed some Aussie blue too

Melbourne's melody*
(2010)

I was taught, pubs are dangerous
Go clubbing, I was taught
where guys grope your arse
and fights fuel the past
where they gather in droves
zombie-dance in drugged monotones
The pubs are dangerous, I was taught
Full of beer-drunks and yobbos
Keep to your kind, I was taught

Go clubbing.
Go clubbing.

Drained from the vein
I tried to find my way
searching through my pain
I refused to play the game
they told me I'm insane

and then you came

My muso, the heartbeat of the city
My muso, the lifeline of bright lights
His electrified blood hums
in unquenchable melodies
drum thrash and guitar riffs
He dresses in the suits of day
teaching students, pulling beers
serving food and scaffolding smiles
my muso counts change
swings a golf club

and aims, for stars

My muso. My muso.

My craving is insatiable
Fanged, I roam, to lights.

Catch me if you can.

The garage grunt of darkened rooms
load in load out load in load out
a voice, bass, guitar, drums
the phantoms of Melbourne's twilight
playing for forty bucks split four ways
ejecting sounds that electrify their insides
the never-ending riffs that occupy the mind
branded like stamps tattooed on a wrist
my muso holds a door open for me
in the strobe lights I couldn't see
what was right there in front of me
I drink from the vein, Melbourne's melody

On sticky carpets within cracked walls
asleep on the stage, snuggling the page
their voices screaming my silenced rage
securely encased, familiarly embraced
my hideaway home, my home inside home
and outside a sizzling BBQ to make it better
casually conversing on sports and the weather
whether or not live music will survive
the next rally or protest to keep it alive

Barefoot my muso bears the brunt
banned from busking for biscuits
in busy Bourke Street bliss
tangled and tripping over wires
compressed into dark corners
you soundproof his sweat
masking-tape his mouth
flood him with your America
unsympathetic you unleash
your psychedelic psychosis
the liquor licence liquorish
one pub down, two clubs open
corporate cathartic contortions
undercover cannabis and cocaine
subsidising race cars and cash cows

Closing your eyes
Killing culture, Casino style

Drained from the vein
we've tried to find our way
searching through our pain
we refuse to play your game
and now Melbourne's gone insane
then you wonder, who's to blame?

New Victorian liquor-licensing laws introduced in late 2009 meant music venues would have to pay up to 500% more to stay open, forcing the closure of many including the iconic The Tote where Koraly would attend regularly when she emancipated herself from her marriage and cultural and religious shackles. Melbourne took to the streets to protest (Koraly wrote this poem), with positive changes to government policy allowing The Tote to reopen six months later. The Tote will turn 42 years old in 2024.

The great Australian dream
(2015)

Get a house, buy a house
Don't worry about living
Save for a house
Work hard, buy a house
I'm sorry, what did you say?
You don't have a house?
This is the land of opportunity!
Rent money is dead money
Get a house, buy a house
Don't stop working, don't breathe
Don't worry about time with the kids
Just get a house, buy a house
It doesn't matter if you
don't like the work you're doing
Get a house, buy a house
I'm sorry did you say you rent?
Next please –
I need to find a suitable father for my kids
Health problems from all the stress?
It will all be worth it in the end
when you are sitting
in your very own
HOUSE
Take your pick –
a corner block or
a house made of sticks
What are you doing?!!!!
Get a job, get a house
Get a house, you fucking loser
You are being so lazy!
Responsibilities! Responsibilities!

Get a better job with longer hours
& it will pave the way to buy a house
Save all your money
You got to save
Save your money *re malaka*
So when you are on your death bed
(don't worry if you got too many regrets)
Because you will have made it
Achieved the great Australian dream
If you die with
YOUR VERY
OWN
HOUSE

Metro nightclub (The Palace)*

How could you take Metro away from me
in the same breath as funding this poem?
How could you do that to us?
Weren't our memories worth enough?
Just to erect yet another hotel?
Curse you, Melbourne, curse you
How could you not understand that
Metro was our liberation, our escape
The only place I danced free
Yet you did not think to protect it

To protect us

When you allowed them to
gutter it, it was as if you
guttered the entire soul of my youth,
that naïve girl that
believed all the world's problems
could be danced away

Now our youth
have nowhere to dance

With three floors of stunning Victorian decorations, The Palace Theatre (1911), became Metro in 1987, featuring in TV shows such as Kath and Kim, its events including techno Fridays (Joy), concerts such as Greek singer Hatzigiannis, and monthly underage daytime dance parties. In 2011 developers took control, Melbourne rallying for a heritage listing. While awaiting the outcome, the developers illegally demolished the beautiful interiors and were fined, but the heritage application was unsuccessful on the grounds that too much damage had been done. Today a lavish hotel stands on Metro's gravesite.

I can stay a bit longer, maybe

Maybe, I can stay a bit longer
extend my trip by an extra week
I can stay a bit longer maybe
keep circling around the same circle
until I stop crying
maybe that would satisfy
the deep craving inside my soul

for more swims
for more beach
for more old town Limassol walks
for more sea

for more me

maybe if I stay a bit longer, maybe

maybe I can close my eyes
when I'm back in Australia
pretend I'm in Cyprus
maybe if I Facebook call my cousin
it will feel like I'm almost there
maybe I'll be able to taste
my favourite *spanakopita*
maybe,
maybe I'll be able to erase
my displacement in Australia
the disdain I feel for the place
and how it's as if it's constantly
trying to expunge me from its land
energetically

Sometimes I think he cursed me
Because he was my first love
& I fell in love with him too young
long before I understood
what 'emotional damage'
really meant

maybe when you fall in love
with a man from the island
the island becomes the love
maybe this is Aphrodite's doing
it is her island after all

I must be cursed
Cursed to belong nowhere
To be caught in a tug of war
Between two places
Cursed to live in a land
I do not belong

Dear parking inspector who just gave me a ticket on Sydney Road
(2013)

Why'd you do that, man?
Seriously, I was only six
minutes past half an hour!
Are you the same guy
who gave me a ticket
on the same strip
a few weeks ago?
I know I should have
parked in the 3 hour
car spots behind
the two dollar shop
opposite Coburg market
but geez, fuck man
I was having a bad day
and I was in a rush
to meet my friend
at Andre's café
where we usually
meet to obsess
about men

Were you watching me or something?
Because I could clearly
see my car from where
we were chatting
You probably got me
when I dashed into
the market to pick up
two cucumbers

Seriously, I mean no disrespect
but how the hell do you sleep at night?
I really don't need yet another
pinch that I need to get
my shit into gear

Fuck man, fuck

I think I'll just leave it at that

You don't even deserve this poem
But this isn't about you is it?
It's about my overwhelming need
to express myself about
every single stupid
thing that happens
so why don't you just
have a big laugh about it
go on, have a big
fucking laugh
about how you gave
some overly neurotic
poet a parking ticket
on Sydney Road
Go on, have a laugh,
you, parking inspector person
laugh, laugh, laugh, laugh,
laugh, laugh, laugh,
laugh, laugh,
laugh

The Literary Judge

I write my poems on the fly

I write my poems on the fly
People think they're unrefined
That I don't spend enough time with them
They're not 'up to scratch'
Not proper poetic form
But, I write my poems on the fly
I'm not some white middle-class guy
who has been educated in literature,
who has been awarded a grant to sit and write
20 to 50 poems
over the space of one year
& work on his craft
& refine and make it perfect
I'm a divorced single mum
from a working-class sexist, patriarchal background
where stomping and looking down on women
is very much quite normal
And everyone, including my family,
doesn't want me to write
They want me to shut my mouth, sew it tight
I'm just trying to survive my circumstances
This isn't me playing the victim
This just me explaining why
my poems are as raw as my heart
& why they are the way they are

So why are you trying to change me?

The literary judge

Submit to me, and I will bestow on you
the highest honour, in all of the Literary Kingdom.
I will determine your   A   R   T
edit your wannas to want tos
wash out your dialect
make you sound more *Australian*
I say what poetry is and *this*, isn't a poem

You will not change the narrative voice
You will not truncate your sentences
You will punctuate correctly
follow all the rules they teach
You will be educated in literature
or else you really needn't bother
We only take *serious* writers seriously
so thank you kindly for your submission
please resubmit at a much later date

I want to shoot Simon Armitage (poet laureate of England)

(A feminist literary metaphorical critique
by the self-appointed Cypriot poet laureate of colonised
Australia)

It's not him I want to shoot, it's his poems
I want to line them up like bottles
at a Texas shooting range
& put a bullet in every one
I want to hear them smash,
to hear them shatter
I want his words blown apart
I want to make a mess with his form
I want him to feel my anger
as I shoot each one
one by one
I want to make him cry
I want to make him feel
I want him to feel so much
he can't do anything but
write a poem that is more than just
conventionally aesthetically pleasing,
one that tears out his heart
& lays it bare and bloody and beating
for all of us to witness

Wog
(2010)

I'll punch it out at you.
Yeah I'm a wog –
and?
Yeah my parents are off the boat –
and?
What are you looking at?
Just 'cause you don't say the word
don't mean it don't exist.
Don't you dare look down at me,
with those condescending eyes,
'cause I'm climbing up there to you –
and past you,
look around you
This is my joint too –
I'm not degraded / just segregated
from you.
This is my joint too –
from the Yarra to the Westgate
from Broadie to your upper class Toorak
from Sydney to Brisbane
This is my joint too –
and I'm not gonna sound like you,
like your intellectual, bland voice,
just to get into your books and your tv and your cinema.
I'm no Peter Carey
I'm no Neighbours barbie either
I'm me. Wog.
Australia's my joint too –
and I'm not going *nowhere*

White wog

YOU
YOU
YOU
You are white
You have white privilege
You white WOG
You dirty, uneducated WHITE WOG
Go back to where you came from, white WOG
Go back to the kitchen and make souvlaki, WOG
You are not relevant anymore, WOG
You've had your day, WOG
You have so much white privilege, you WOG
No solidarity to you sister
Too olive for mainstream appeal
Your white privilege is unbelievable
You've had your day, WOG
You're out of our circle, WOG
Get out, WOG
Get out, WOG
GET OUT

Ashamed of my art
(2014)

There are many times a day
where I am confronted with
the shame that is my art
Maybe someone else
would find it a lot easier

People look at me
think it is easy

A guy I once dated
who I am still friends with
tells me I can't be in a
relationship

It would affect my art

Is art my love?
I doubt it
I hate it

Yet I don't abandon it

I have tried
many times before

But I stay in the end

I don't want to be
in this relationship

Are you a writer?

If you are a writer,
you may need
to ask yourself

am I a puppet or
a writer?

Puppet has become
the new hipster,
as the literati chink
their glasses,
the panellists
keep their seats warm
for the next round,
pull down their pants,
ready to hand out new badges
to the most critically acclaimed kissers

If you are a writer, ask yourself:
Do you write what you really think?
Do you sound like everybody else?
Do you try to mould and shape shift
present yourself like a present to
the mainstream?

Mainstream left
or the mainstream right
it's really the same thing,
clinging to the safety
of solidarity,
for argument's sake

Sure, there's safety in numbers
We all want to get paid
Best to pick a side
& stick to it
But ask yourself,
are you perpetuating problems
to stay clicked into the clique
for the glory of retweets?

Both the left and the right,
they don't want change,
they just want to stay
stuck in their ways
I wonder sometimes:
Do I live inside a fairy-tale snow-globe
because I hope for change?

They'll try to burn you
at the stake from both sides
if you go out on a limb
Be fearless, be bold
You may think the cost is too great,
but if we all don't rise up and speak,
say what we really think,
humanity will have to
foot the silence
instead

Burnt bridges
(2014)

I tell my sis
that I think
I've burnt bridges
publishing a poem
about the Aus Lit
industry & that
I will probably
never get published
in this country

& she says

why'd you do it for then?

& I say

I don't know...
maybe because deep down
I don't want to be successful
and I want to stop writing
because I'm tired and maybe
so I can please my family
and stay a computer programmer

& we all burst into laughter
& my sis starts clapping yay!
& I go over and hug her
coz I love her so much
& she has the cutest cheeks

& my bro says

he says

look, Koz (because that's my nick)

he says Koz

you know I love ya
but my only advice to you is
chase the dollar
because that's
what pays the bills
& you'll be happy
you'll have a house
and security, you know?

Yeah, I know…

Don't worry, I'll go

I am going, somewhere
to Cyprus, where I belong
and I am sure you will be
relieved when I am gone

I am too loud for you anyway
& sometimes I honestly
can't bothered climbing
your tall walls

fighting racism with racism
you started it
so we fought back
then you fought back
& we fought back
& now it's hard to recall
why it all began

It's not even your land anyway
but don't worry, I'll go
& I know you won't miss me
Maybe I'll miss you, sometimes
I might miss your coldness
as I walk along Cyprus
endless Mediterranean blue
with golden heat enveloping me
on my way to the beach
on my lunch break
almost time for siesta
& I'll think

how stressed out you made me
for most of my life
how a group of Aussie boys
picked on me at primary school
& how Mum and Dad didn't
call it racism, just said
I had to learn to be strong

Yeah, I might think of you

sometimes

My café residency kicked me out
(2012)

My poetry is palpable
Maybe I should stop writing
I went into my café yesterday
and my books, my shoebox mailbox –
they were all under the counter

Maybe I shouldn't be a poet

The lovely manager who agreed to my residency
isn't coming back. She left the country temporarily
to renew her visa but was stopped at customs

I'm starting to think this isn't just bad luck

The new manager in charge was telling me
that she doesn't think my residency
was cleared with upper management.
That's when it all started making sense:
How my naughty folder, where I keep
my censored poetry, went missing
How some of my poetry books disappeared

I want to stop writing!
This café is like a shrine to you!

When I opened my shoebox mailbox I had two letters
One was a lovely poem about life,
the other went something along the lines of
(It's not word for word because I threw
the paper in the bin immediately after reading):

Honestly I think your poetry is shit.
Please refrain from vomiting your words
all over the tables with your poetry cards
And beside the letter was one of my poetry cards
all scrunched up that read:
I fluctuate between loving you and crucifying you

The new manger thinks her manager
doesn't want poetry in the café anymore
but she'll let me know

I'm pretty sure my café is kicking me out

Later that night, my mobile chimes triumphantly:
Koraly, I'm sorry but we won't be requiring you
to come in anymore. We are really sorry.

Why can't I just write normal academic poetry?
Why can't it all just be flowers and trees?
Why does it have to be completely fucked?
Why can't I stop writing about you?

And once again, my poetry is homeless,
trying to find a café – pub – bar – corner
to call home, but

I am thinking early retirement is the best option

Being brave

I don't want to be brave anymore
I want to be quiet
I am tired
I want to sleep
This isn't me giving in
This is me making a choice –
choosing the other path in the fork
instead of the one I stupidly walked down
It's harder than I thought it would be – being brave
It's time consuming and costs a lot
Bravery is pricey
& it never really evens out
Now I understand why the majority
              of the population plays it safe
do their 9 – 5 job
              and their 5 – 9 marriage
+ 1 car + 2 kids
              and a mortgage
Why not?
Let someone else expose their bruised wounds
for others to feast on
Let someone else be brave for the benefit of others
I'm tired. I want to sleep, eat and be merry

A Fucking Arsehole-Of-A-Man Killed His Wife

Your opinions

Thank you for your pitch,
but unfortunately
we're going to have to pass
Or not respond
Thank you for writing on spec
Although we showed
much enthusiasm initially
we're going have to PASS on you
& your middle-class female views
We've already got an
ethnic male writer on staff
We've done all the right things,
ticked all our white boxes
You're too loud anyway
& we might upset
our advertisers

Please go write
a poem
instead

Community TV choking*
(2014)

Hey! Mr Turnbull
Minister of miscommunication
I have something to say to YOU

I may be a Good Greek Girl
I may have been marginalised and silenced
and stitched up till I can't breathe,
but I exploded out of all that

I am one angry Greek Girl
and I am coming for YOU
Wild hair, stiletto boots
a whip and chain
of my very own too

So let's start talking

Must feel good, to have your hands
wrapped around Channel 31's neck,
your sweaty palms, pressing hard,
restricting the airway minute by minute,
stopping the airflow, killing art
that doesn't fit into your squeaky clean
unchallenged, white, middle-class existence

must feel good to stop actors and writers like me
pushing through, must feel great to put
the marginalised in their place
because who needs shows like
Vasili's Plant Farm & *Legally Brown*
when you can watch

The Bachelor
& Big Brother
This is real Australia
We don't need to learn anything other than
how to bitch and be pretentious
and aspire to be white just like you

Is Australia not mainstream enough for you?
Not white enough?
Not home shopping enough?
Not American enough?
Not male dominated enough?
Not #TeamAustralia enough for you?

Doors keep shutting all around me
My culture wants me to shut up
& it seems you want me to shut up too
Where do I belong?
In your mind, where does my art fit in?
In the #TeamAustralia picture in your mind
where do I feature?
Do I feature at all?
Or would you rather ignore me?
Should I stay behind the kitchen sink where I belong
rather than have my poetry on TV?
rather than inspiring other women to break free?

How disheartening it is
to see my image
erased away
one policy at a time
Keep going, Mr Turnbull
Keep erasing and erasing us
until your hand tires

& there is nothing
on Australian shelves
but stale
white
bread

Former Prime Minister of Australia, Malclom Turnbull (2015-2018) was Minister of Communication (2013-2015) before he challenged the then Prime Minister Tony Abbott, overthrowing him and taking his position.

Channel 31 is Victoria's only community television station based in Melbourne and broadcasts Australia-wide. Several governments have tried to axe it but due to much activism, it still runs today and provides emerging television practitioners and artists opportunities to present their work.

Deciphering the Arts Minister's speech
(2015)

'In addressing the lack of
cultural diversity present
in our Arts sector,
within this elitist
& conservative
One Australian Nation
which we exist in today,
where the majority of prizes & funding
are awarded to smart white boys
and pretty white girls that
can write well but have
dead shit boring stories
yet are easily transferrable
across this white supremacist world
we live in today,
where everyone not white
sits firmly under the thumb
of all the true white nations,
I, the intelligent Arts Minister,
who belongs to a party of
right-wing bigots,
plan to remove a big chunk
of arms-length funding power
Australia Council has
and give it to myself
and my ministry to dish out
to art that is to the tastes
of this great Australian white nation,
but particularly books and films and theatre
which can be enjoyed with glass of chardonnay,

out in the Australian country side,
art that is pleasant to take in,
easy to understand
and keeps this
great white world
as it should be.'

Oil-petrol-gas*

We all know that oil-petrol-gas
makes the world go round
It was just our luck
that we found it on our doorstep,
the one we share with unwelcome regimes

No offence to the Turkish Cypriots
I see you just like one of us,
but your government is not you
It was a government outside you
that came in to claim half our land
in the name of you
nothing to do with you
other than speaking your language,
for you are not Turkey, you are Cyprus,
and we are not Greece, we are Cyprus

So then, foreign government, Turkey,
it's bad enough you came in
to create all this mess
under the guise of
'saving people',
not only did you have the audacity
to create a republic on land you have no right to,
but now you think you have a claim
to the oil-petrol-gas of our land

It's like – wow
Just wow
Are you that selfish?
I suppose so

Are you that dumb?
Is seems so

The international community
keep telling you that you
have no rights to our land
that you never did,
that you are illegally occupying it,
but you keep building up your army
keep sending out your drill ships,
you don't seem like a government
interested in peace,
you are like a spoilt child
who wants and takes and still wants

It just astounds me, the audacity of your actions
We are not interested in war
Maybe we should just let you take the pump
Maybe we should shove it up your arse
Watch your ego balloon even more
Maybe that would satisfy you?

I doubt it

There is no child, quite like you, Turkey
Most of the Turkish Cypriots –
the original ones,
not the ones you shipped over from Turkey
to increase your numbers
(don't think we didn't notice) –
They don't even like you!

You are like a child who constantly
needs a dummy shoved in its mouth
Cypriots are not like you
We are nothing like you
So why don't you just fuck off
Go back to where you came from
And leave us all in peace

Turkey has been illegally occupying northern Cyprus since 1974. Cyprus was once an English colony but was only granted independence in 1960 under certain conditions: 1.England always retain their military bases on our land; 2.England, Turkey and Greece always remain guarantors of the island.

Cyprus has seen a number of sizable gas discoveries since 2011, with local newspaper Phileleftheros *reporting in 2019 gas reservoirs recently discovered by US oil giant ExxonMobil may be worth $30-40 billion. However, Cyprus has not been able to exploit these reserves and is relying on other countries, like Greece and Israel, as reported in* Reuters *on September 5th, 2023.* The German Marshall Fund of the United States *stated in their March 2015 paper* 'Gas discoveries in the Eastern Mediterranean: Implications for Regional Maritime Security': *"Large offshore gas discoveries in the Eastern Mediterranean could have a profound impact on the region's energy, economic, and geopolitical future…a number of maritime delimitation disputes complicate the exploration and development of the resources…the state of war between Lebanon and Israel, the conflict between Israel and the Palestinians, the Cyprus question, and the strained relations between Turkey and Israel. The Republic of Cyprus, "the Turkish Republic of North Cyprus," Turkey, Israel, and Lebanon have all staked claims in the gas fields, some of which conflict with or raise legal objections from other parties. This situation has a negative impact on maritime security in the region."*

The Cypriot rape case*
(2020)

En gini bou bige sto domatio me ena botiri betrelleo
E, kalo, ti berimenis? Ego bantos den xehno**
En I Englezi bou mas viasan brota
Brebi na timorithi. I gineka brebi na timorithi
Oi kale, nomizi eho ibomoni gia noumera
Enge birazi me an klapsi
Enge birazi me an travmatisti
Enge birazi me oute kan
I hora mas dipsa

She's the one who went to the bedroom
    with a glass of petrol
Well, what did you expect?
I certainly won't forget**
It's the English that raped us first
They need to be punished
The English woman needs to be punished
She thinks we all have the patience for drama
I don't care if she weeps or if she's traumatised
I don't care one bit
Our country is thirsty

Text in traditional Cypriot dialect, written with English characters. English translation below. The poem refers to a high-profile case in 2019 of an allegation by an English tourist who reported rape by 12 Israeli students. They were interrogated and released, the woman charged for public mischief. This decision was overturned in 2022.

**den xehno "I won't forget" is the phrase used by Cypriots on the 20th of July to mark the anniversary of the 1974 invasion by Turkish forces, which many believe was a direct result of English colonisation.

What are you wearing to the Melbourne Cup?*

Are you wearing a hat?
Or are you wearing blood on your hands?
I wore a hat when I was twenty-three
when I was completely naïve,
my husband on my hand like an accessory

We were in a corporate marquee
We drank champagne, ate canopies
Another time we had a picnic
& I won some money
betting on the horses
like all the uncles did
when I was growing up
every weekend

But as the day progressed
there were more and more people drunk around me,
staggering home in their stilettos
Australia's public pride
The race that stops a nation

And it very-well should stop the nation,
these beautiful, sturdy, athletic horses
It better stop the nation
Now that we know the truth
Australia pumping out 14,000 horses a year
to try and find the next Melbourne Cup winner
Slaughtering at least 4,000 a year
when they're not good enough
Not only slaughtering them
but torturing them
Shooting bolts into their heads

Electrocuting them
Leaving them to lay there and die
& shouting at them in the most degrading ways
Killing them in the most inhumane ways possible
Watch the *7:30* report investigation on the ABC
You'll see it with your own eyes
Horses being killed and sold off as food
to other countries, for humans, for pets

But it's the Melbourne Cup
The fashion parade, the models and their outfits
Oaks Day, Darby Day, Cup Day – take your pick
What famous singer is singing this year?
This sport makes breeders and hardworking Australians
thousands and thousands of dollars
We get a public holiday so our children learn to play

Out with the old horses, in with the new
Got to keep the production line going
to satisfy the great Australian appetite for sport
Who cares about ethics?
Ethics make me feel uncomfortable
We just want to have a great day
at the marquee, sipping champagne
What are you wearing to the cup this year?
A fascinator? A new outfit from Myer?
A lovely handbag to go with your side of horse?
Of course, you'll go with that hat
And lots of blood on your hands…

Dubbed 'the race that stops a nation', Melbourne Cup is part of Melbourne's Spring Racing Carnival. It is one of the biggest horse racing events in the world and has been a public holiday since 1876.

Louie, Louie, Louie*
(for Louie CK, 2017)

Louie, Louie, Louie, Louieeeee
Louie, Louie, Louie, Louwhyyy
Louie, Louie, Louie, Louieeeee
Louie, Louie, you made all the girls cry

Louie, Louie, Louie why did you play
Play, play, play the predicable male power game
Louie, Louie, Louie I wanted to be your wife
Louie, Louie, Louie now your career's gonna die

Louie, Louie, Louie you broke my heart today
Your comedy was such an ode to honesty
It inspired me in so many ways
Louie I always wanted to hear what you had to say

Louie why did you wave your magic wand
    at your colleagues?
In the arts world that is like doing it in a workplace
If I was around maybe that could have been me
Louie, Louie, Louie I think I would have been pretty scared

Louie, Louie, Louie there are cliques
Cliquey, cliquey arty cliques
If people speak out they are shut out
Of the industry, the arts and their careers

Louie, Louie, Louie you broke my heart today
I want to cry for you, Louie, for being such a dick
The world is truly a very ugly place
Famous men falling like dominoes and nowhere is safe

Louie, Louie, Louie, Louieeeee
Louie, Louie, Louie, Louwhyyy
Louie, Louie, Louie, Louieeeee
Louie, Louie, you made the whole world cry

Louis C.K. was one of Koraly's most treasured comedians and TV show creators, who was lorded for his vulnerability and honesty, until a few of his female co-workers came forward alleging he would masturbate in front of them without their consent.

Thank you, feminist Gillard*
(2012)

The Centrelink** queue is weaving
around the bend this afternoon
It's Friday and I'm not the only one craving
getting my life sorted before the weekend,
contemplate turning away but
it took me four hours of

mind looping

to get off the couch
so I tack to the end of the crim line
little one resting on stomach,
she keeps asking me
what 'exactly' Centrelink is

kids run around unhinged
a single mum that fits the stereotype
people are thinking she should
learn to control her kids
so she complies, yells in her child's face
and now people are thinking

She is a Bitch

but all I hear is the screech
sounds like the hold message
on Centrelink's phone line:
'if you are a single parent calling
about your parenting payment being cut cut cut
please press one NOW'

There is a cute guy in the queue
resembles the only guy I have ever
fallen in love-at-first-sight with
spoke to me for hours at a bar
asked if I'd like to go for coffee
across the road
Yes! Let's go for coffee!
Okay, just wait here, I'll be back in a minute...
but he never came back
and I'm still waiting

I contemplate going up to this guy,
asking him to marry me
but then I'd just end up
right back where I started

yet maybe repression
isn't so bad
maybe things like
rape, abuse and neglect
aren't so bad when you
have a husband
money and roof
for you and your kids

Centrelink is in a state of disadvantage and disorganisation,
maybe a consequence of allowing a childless
    anti-misogynist feminist
to run the country

Single mums should feel empowered
by this new wave of feminism,
by Gillard's iconic, empowering speech
We should stitch up our vaginas because

aren't there enough kids in the world, already?

I am proud to be Australian, standing in this crim line,
received my government grant a few weeks ago
then got my parenting payment cut in half
even though I'm not allowed to spend the money

on living

but then I was told all would be okay
they would give me back my payment
just until I find a part-time
new-Gillard-participation-requirements
'résumé' type job, and no
'art' does not count

The government gives at one end, cuts at the other

so I try to squeeze words out of my non-existent time to
write this poem to give single mums a voice since Gillard
has further compressed their time to just the air they
breathe and so now I try to write between looking for a
job, taking my little one to the doctors, the optometrist,
psychologist, pick up and drop off from school,
homework, grocery shopping, clean the house, pay the bills,
play time, cuddle time, rent or mortgage push and pull all
while trying my hardest to produce art encouraging
repressed women to

break free

Dear Feminist Gillard,
I would like to apply for the position of motherhood. If you have any vacancies in your cabinet, please do inform me as I am very much interested in taking care of my daughter.

Yours sincerely
Koraly Dimitriadis
(Australia Council recipient)

I think feminist Gillard might actually prefer
my daughter feels even more heartbroken and neglected
than she already does after her family spilt up
bouncing between two houses like a ping pong ball
otherwise why would she be forcing
single parents to go back to work full time
when they're oldest child is eight?

I think feminist Gillard prefers I palm off my child
to before-and-after-school care
and have her crying and having bad dreams
because she misses and wants her mummy

I think feminist Gillard prefers I take pills
& shut the fuck up
or else why cut the number of visits
allowed to see a psychologist?

I think feminist Gillard prefers that I'm homeless
Or maybe I should kill myself and be just another
single mum, drugged fucked slut casualty

I think feminist Gillard might just prefer
I didn't have a child at all

Maybe we should kill all bastard children
    & be done with it?
Then the government can have their surplus and *everyone*
can sleep better at night that taxes aren't being spent on
single mum dole bludgers that keep having kids to stay on
the poverty line pension

Suddenly repression is looking, inviting.

Thank you, feminist Gillard
Thank you, from one woman to another
Thank you

Prime Minister Julia Gillard (2010-2103) was Australia's first and only female Prime Minister, today heralded by feminists for her iconic anti-misogyny speech delivered to parliament on October 9th 2012. It was also the same day she changed the law putting single mothers at further disadvantage, but this was largely ignored by the media and is still ignored today by many feminists.

**Centrelink: Australia's social services

Pauline Hanson to chair a senate inquiry into the broken family law system
(2019)

It's not every day you get out of bed and want to vomit
The nausea came the night before on the news
Family Law overhaul and Pauline Hanson to manage it all
I've never felt so sick, something like
a woman being punched in the gut by her ex-husband
then watching him take away her child for the week

Misogynist, senator Pauline Hanson
Done her deal with Prime Minister Morrison
Children cry in their cribs

They're crying because
the system that was built to protect their wellbeing,
the flawed rule introduced of 50/50 shared parenting,
that's going to get even further smashed by her
She's going to get out her past experience,
her son being accused of domestic violence
and not having access to his kids
She's going to break that glass down into shards
so they're wedged everywhere in our society

She says the system works against men
But how can that be when they usually
    have the most money?
How are the women supposed to fight for their children
when they stopped working to care for them
while the men continued to climb off their backs?
How are the women supposed to fight for their children
when Legal Aid won't even qualify them for help?

Australian family law, a system made for the rich
The divorce lawyers ride in, promise to provide shelter
to vulnerable women seeking help, answers and protection
Shrug their shoulders after the money's run dry
Quietly walk away

I ask you who the hell is going to take care of our children?
The ones who see their mums bashed
The ones that see their mums scared
The ones who get bashed by their fathers
The ones who get murdered by them?

Who is going to protect the child
who goes back and forth between parents
between fighting and arguing
Who is going to protect this child
from psychological trauma?
Who is going to sacrifice what the parent wants
and what the parent needs to give this child stability?

And let's not forget the gag order
that prevents anyone who enters the family law system
from ever going public about what goes on

What goes on behind closed doors
Stays behind closed doors
What goes on behind closed doors
Stays behind closed doors

The family law system in tatters
Women dying. Children dying
Scott Morrison's got his meal ticket
And I guess that's all that matters

In the name of justice, fairness, and victims of child sex abuse*
(2020)

Cardinal, your letter reads like you think
    you're a messenger from God
Make no mistake, it was a technicality that set you free
Your expensive lawyers may be able to argue to
    the nth degree
But in this poem, I'm in charge, and you won't go free

Sit in silence for a while,
    read your judgment while we all vomit
You've had a long time to write your just-in-case prayer
Sentences as carefully crafted as lies
Will you have your lawyers come after me?
Judge me with defamation?
Blessed are those who donated to the church, hey?
Funded you to do your bidding
Please do not pass on your tainted concerns to the public
    in this pandemic
Your hand is the hand of the damned
You must feel as powerful as God
For what you've accomplished here
Turned the legal institutions inside out
Maintained your innocence to the end
You talk of truth, but there is only one truth
A truth that you are perhaps too deranged to see
Only a sick, twisted man would hurt a child,
and it's that same sick, twisted man that takes the stand
Kneel before us and confess your sins
The only injustice suffered here is not your own
But of all the victims of the church,

not just the sex abuse victims,
but all the people who have been hurt by the church,
who have their lives plagued by the church,
    and it's teachings
You may be out on the streets, walking free,
but we all see you and your patriarchal institution
    for what it is
We renounce it like you do Satan
I spit on you, and the religious followers
    and institutions that cloak your sin
This isn't over yet, justice will be awarded one day
In the meantime, think of this as Hell
I sentence your soul to an eternity in this poem
Feel my rage, and burn

Cardinal George Pell, secretary for the Vatican, and the most senior Catholic cleric in Australia, was convicted of child sex abuse in 2019 and of hiding the sexual abuse of other priests, but the decision was overturned in 2020. Pell died suddenly in 2023 during hip replacement surgery.

A fucking arsehole-of-a-man killed his wife
(For Hannah Clarke)

A fucking arsehole-of-a-man killed his wife
A fucking arsehole psycho-piece-of-shit killed his wife
Not a 'family man' or a 'top bloke'
Why don't the media tell it like it is?
A fucking arsehole-of-a-man killed his wife
And his kids. His three beautiful kids
A fucking arsehole-of-a-man killed his wife

A fucking arsehole-of-a-man could pose for the camera
His hand around her throat behind the scenes
He was not part of a perfect family
There is no need to establish how it was perfect
& then how it all went wrong
A fucking arsehole-of-a-man was controlling
He was insane enough to
Blow up his own kids
There is nothing to decipher here
He wasn't a good guy
No need to uncover what went wrong
A fucking arsehole psycho-piece-of-shit killed his wife
He was nothing but a monster
   she was trying to get away from
Who believes a woman anyway, until it's too late
He didn't kill his 'family'
He lost the right to that word
when he doused those beautiful people in petrol
& insisted they continue to burn when people tried to help
A fucking arsehole-of-a-man killed his wife
It isn't a shock that we need to uncover
No need to use the word 'alleged' he is fucking dead
A fucking arsehole-of-a-man killed his wife

This monster was just really good at being fake to the rest
 of the world
Just because he could force her smile at the camera
Doesn't mean he wasn't a controlling cunt
 behind the scenes
A fucking arsehole-of-a-man killed his wife

Missing in Brunswick (Part II)*
(For Jill Meagher, 2012)

Jill, I think, I'm obsessed with you
I google for updates at least once a day
watch the mainstream news every night
I know you're somewhere out there
but I am not sure if you are alive or…
in a warehouse in Brunswick somewhere
underneath floorboards
breathing final breaths
wish I had a magic camera
I'd zoom into all the
abandoned places
crannies and spaces
got to try and find
got to try and find try
harder harder to find you

Jill, I study your image
you are all of my fears
dressed up elegantly to meet the night
you are girl-in-love eyes
before innocence meets its demise
reality's reflection
shattering the contradiction
of life, and safety – what are we?

My mum is lecturing me
that I should move myself and my daughter
back into her house, strip myself of my freedom
because some cunt of a man
needs to have his dick severed

Jill, I watched the CCTV footage, we all have
We've all had weirdo guys approach us
try to be amicable, we don't want to
piss them off who knows what they'll do
pretend you're waiting for a friend
or call family on the phone
casually walk away, pray,
tell yourself, promise yourself
you'll be more careful next time
don't make a big deal out of it
because it might escalate
into something out of your control

When your weirdo guy approached
looks like he touched your hair
how fucking dare he
how fucking dare anyone touch you
without your fucking permission
in your hood, on your turf
in your Brunswick
you were only 400m from your house
still on Sydney Road you called your brother
pretended like people knew you were out
that they were expecting you at home
kept on your way, towards home
but that didn't seem to deter him

Oh, Jill, sweetheart
It was the pot luck of the draw
He was pacing up and down
waiting for you or someone like you
He saw you. He saw you, Jill
His gaze sank its fangs into your beauty
Jill, if you lived on Sydney Road

you might have made it home
It's the pot luck of the draw
that your house was in a laneway
just off Hope Street
Your problem was that you had to
walk down Hope Street to get home,
narrow, dimly lit, Hope Street
Parting with Sydney Road safety
your senses dampened with drinks
it would have been like one of those dreams
where you are trying to scream
and nothing comes out

Oh, Jill, sweetheart
The clock has struck 12
Time is running out
I am praying they find you safe
and I am not even religious
The pot luck of the fucking draw!
If only you didn't have to walk down Hope Street
If only you didn't have to walk down Hope Street
If only we all didn't have to walk down Hope Street

Part one of this poem is published in Koraly's second poetry book, Just Give Me The Pills. *The three poems were written as events unfolded over the space of a few weeks. Jill was murdered in vibrant Brunswick where many Greek migrants arrived in the 70s and still live. In more recent times, Brunswick has attracted many artists, creating a kaleidoscope of culture. Jill's perpetrator was on parole for a number of sexual offenses when he randomly attacked her, raping and strangling her a few streets from Koraly's home, burying her body out in bushland. He was arrested and is currently serving a life sentence.*

Part III: Death in Brunswick

I do not want you to be dead
I do not want you to be dead

Like the heavy black cape
you were wearing that night,
your soul blankets Brunswick
We're operating a little slower today
as we jaywalk across Sydney Road
your spirit lingers in our eyes
exchange sympathetic glances
with residents we've never met
a sombre, bitter-relief kind of peace
the clouds have gathered
it's raining non-stop
forecast says it's going
to get really cold

Turns out you may have never made it to Hope Street, Jill
I'm trying to get there, not sure if I can, will
I cut off unnecessary words from my Facebook Page
changed the title from 'Koraly Dimitriadis
    – Love and F**k Poems'
to just 'Koraly Dimitriadis' FULL STOP so it's boy short
Don't want anyone to touch me right now

Death walks in Brunswick
can't see it, a figure of a man, ghost-like
lock your doors, double check, once, twice
tuck in my baby girl for the night
refrain from projecting into the future
don't feel any safer with the arrest
think about moving, not too sure

where safe is anymore

Your husband and brother sit in court
Want to be face-to-face
We're all sitting behind them
All of Brunswick are in the front rows
Behind them, the rest of the northern suburbs
Behind them, the remainder of Melbourne
We all want to hear the words
Want justice to be served
Want to understand
We want questions answered
How it is possible that you have ceased to breathe
How it is possible that your rights as a woman
to walk freely in your home suburb
just a mere few metres from your house, were violated,
for not only was your body raped and murdered
but your rights were raped
Brunswick's lifestyle was raped
all of Melbourne's rights were raped
all of womankind's rights were raped
and murdered, and buried in a grave out bush

I'd like to stand in the court room crowd
scream out to the highest of judges
demand that the nightmare be undone
take steps back, have Jill go back back
back in time till she is alive
have the justice served back then
when Jill was asleep in her bed, safe and sound

I was brought up in a sheltered wog family
Barely enough experience before marriage
When it was all over I was finally free

To live the life I had always dreamed
Come and go as I pleased

Today, I realise
My eyes were only half open
Could only see the thrill of freedom
Thought my eyes were open wide
Turns out my eyes were wide shut
Today, my eyes have been pried wide
There are boogie-men that indeed lurk in the night
Can't plead with them, can't reason with them
They actually take pleasure in taking your life

Jill, sweetheart, angel
I do not want you to be dead
You could have been my friend
You could have been me
I wish you were safe in bed, asleep
I wish you were having ice-cream on Lygon Street
I wish you were having drinks at The Retreat
Jill, I did not want you to be dead
I did not want you to be dead
I did not want you to be dead
Rest in peace, my beloved friend
We will not forget,
and fight, we will
to the end

Aiia's poem*
(2019)

Aiia, I keeping hearing your head hit the pavement,
down by the mouth of Latrobe,
where the muzzas** and the wogs
got their uni degrees

I keep hearing your head hit hard
You were on the phone to your sis,
if only she could have reached through the line
to strangle him
punch him
stop him
I can hear her screams from Palestine:
Bring my sister's body to me!
Bring her home to me now!

I'd sacrifice knowing your name and your joyous face
just to have you carry on living life like you were,
making the most of all it had to offer you,
being ambitious, reaching for your dreams
riding the ride of life with a smile

Your dreams are our sadnesses now
Your hopes, our heartbreak
Your safety, our nightmare

I always tell the ones who come here
bedazzled by the fruits of Australian opportunity:
Do not be deceived by what you see
There is a bloody history here
Years and years of corrupt policy,

of sexism, racism and misogyny
There is danger in the night
Take care, stay close to others
Be wary, there is danger in the night

I wish I could have told you, Aiia
Maybe then, just maybe, I would not know your name
I wish it was safer for you, that murder
    did not roam in our place
Instead, I keep hearing your head hit the pavement
Aiia, I wish I did not have to write this poem
I wish I did not know your name

Aiia Maasarwe was a Palestinian international exchange student at Latrobe University in Melbourne, known in the 90s/2000s for its huge demographic of students from southern-European migrant backgrounds. She was murdered in 2019 in a violent attack as she returned to her campus dorm from a comedy show.

** muzza: a stereotypical slang term born in the 90s to describe males born in Melbourne from southern-European backgrounds. Traits include driving low-lying, wide cars like Commodores, blasting techno music through subwoofer speakers, frequently attending nightclubs, gelled hairstyles, and wearing branded tracksuits as daywear.

I don't want a gun

I live in Australia
and I don't want a gun
The murders and rapes
were in the hundreds this year
But I still don't want a gun

Trump says a gun is what I need
to keep me safe
But I still don't want a gun
He gets up in front of the NRA
performs his cleverly crafted poetry
perfectly punctuated pauses
He terrifies his audience with
'Others want to take away your guns'
But I still don't want a gun

He presents a woman
who shot an intruder
while her child slept in her room
The crowd applauds
But I still don't want a gun
He showcases a man
who stopped a mass shooting
But I still don't want a gun
He steps up yet another
and another example
of how guns kill
dangerous people with guns
But I still don't want a gun

I don't want a gun
I don't want a gun
Trump, listen to me
Listen to my words
I don't want a gun

He vomits his racism
and another white supremacist takes a gun
He grooms parents
and their child steals the gun
Here in Australia, the laws are tight
and we are fine with that
If I'm going to die
then I'm going to die
and my time is up
But until then I don't want to live
with the fear of bullets eating my insides

I want the guns locked away
Away from the people
Away from our children
Away from this world

Trump stop shoving
your money guns
down my throat

I don't want a gun
I still don't want a gun
Trump, listen to me
Listen to my words:

I don't want your gun

Thin

Like a political pawn

Like a political pawn
they play chess with
our bodies
in exchange for
a glass of petrol

Party

I see a guy
in a heavy metal T-shirt
& I think:
Where has my party spirit gone?
Maybe it was hijacked
by single mum stress
Maybe layers of illness took it away
It could have been striped-searched by establishments,
questioned to the point of exhaustion
Now all that remains is tiredness
I used to dance a long time ago
I haven't forgotten
That's what's so hard about it

Into the light
(2011)

You figured me out quickly
My husband of ten years
didn't even get close
But you forced me into the light
tore off my clothes
ripped off my skin
and like a vampire
exposed to sunlight
I cried out in fright
the disgust of our bodies
I begged for darkness
but you were relentless
said this is the way it had to be
that if we were going to do this
that if we were going to do 'us'
then this is the way, it had to be
but I couldn't stand, I couldn't breathe,
I can't stand, I can't breathe
but you held my hands
would not let me sink
held me close to your body
the hideousness of our skin
and I cried out
You don't understand
You can't understand
And you said *you understand*
No, you don't understand
I understand
You don't
I understand
Ssh…ssh…I understand

There is a dark part of me
(2013)

There is a dark part of me
that people don't see
there is a dark part of me
that lives and breathes
deep in the dungeons
locked inside me
There is a dark part of me
There is a dark part of me

There is a dark of me
that rustles the midnight trees
a flicker, a flash, a burning memory
you, and your warm summer eyes
hovering above and over me

In the light I smile
people talk to me
I am shy, I am mild
and pleasant to see
they bubble with joy
the words that come from me
I am light, I am bright
and courteous and free

but behind my doors
the darkness calls
it pushes, it rushes
it sniggers and claws
I push it to the floor
but it clenches its jaw
demanding to be witnessed

demanding to be called
it has only been seen
by one mere dark soul
only by yours, only by yours

and when we collide
your darkness and mine
our souls scream
hysterically in the night
it isn't agony, but insane delight
denying this darkness
eradicates our light
for darkness like this
must be balanced by light
we never meet in the daylight
it's always in the night

There is a dark part of me that will always be
I see it in you, you see it in me
can we unveil it to others
what we alone have been privy to see?
unravel our fears till we're finally free?
or is my darkness only visible
to you and yours to me?
should we resign to the fact
that we will never be free?
or should I drag my darkness
kicking and screaming
lock it deep inside me
will it disappear out of sight?
or will it eventually
extinguish my light?

There is a dark part of me
that people don't see
there is a dark part of me
that lives and breathes
deep in the dungeons
locked inside me
There is a dark part of me
There is a dark part of me

She's crazy, she's nuts

That chick's crazy
So is that chick &
that chick &
all the chicks I've dated – you say

But hang on a minute,
you made me go crazy too!
Did you ever stop to think
that you're the one
that's making them go crazy?

Or maybe not 'crazy',
maybe you are just
h-u-r-t-i-n-g
t-h-e-m
& they are expressing the pain
you cannot
because you're a guy
& you've been
conditioned not to
do that

Maybe they are acting 'crazy'
because they're carrying two loads,
just like they do when they carry a baby
They are carrying two sets of emotions
that have been churning like lava
only to explode like a volcanic eruption

Maybe you should thank these chicks for their time
& putting up with your shit

The free IUD

Once it's up there, in your uterus,
you just don't know what it's doing
You just don't know – until it's too late
Until you're in hospital
And you can't talk
And you can't move
It's free, in New Zealand
Jacinda Ardern made a pact
But you just don't know
They say it's just like a stone, in your uterus,
blocking the way of the sperm
That it's been around since forever
That they've used it in cows
To stop them from conceiving
They make it seem ingenious
But you just don't know
You don't know what it's doing up there
Until it's too late
Your vagina has a delicate balance of flora and fauna
If that gets thrown out of whack
who knows what will happen to your garden
They tell you pelvic inflammatory disease is a risk
It's in the small print
So you're signing away your rights away
when the doctor makes you aware,
tells you it's 'relatively' safe
& sticks it up there
When the weird stuff starts happening,
they say your body just needs to settle down,
that this foreign object just needs to befriend your body
& then it's smooth sailing from there

But that might take one, two, three years
In the meantime
You just don't know
You don't know what it's doing
What it's controlling
What it's harming
Until you're in a hospital bed
With a drip
And you can't talk, or walk, or be touched
Your body waged a war with the object
Your body didn't want to be friends with it at all
And they tell you you have pelvic inflammatory disease
And they tell you you have fibromyalgia
And you can't walk from here to there
So you just don't know
Until you're on an aeroplane
And you blow up like a balloon
And they tell you 'sorry'
The infection damaged your lymph nodes
Permanently
And you have lymphedema
Oops

I love all the marketing
How it's questionable if the pill is safe
It was okay before the IUD came along
Now we have a new saviour
Choose your flavour
Copper or hormonal
Like slaves to the pharma companies
Like drones to the pharma companies
You can't choose an abortion
Patriarchy wants you to choose something
Or shut your legs, slut

They like to pump us full of hormones
To control our bodies
And then turn around
and call us
all mad

Thin
(2019)

A long time ago, I was thin
So thin
Now I'm fat
I hate my body
It disgusts me
The bulges
What man would love this?
When I don't even want it
& it's mine?
How did it get to this?
Where has my young, healthy body gone?
I don't understand
I try to lose it
It doesn't go
Lymphatic fluid is stubborn
It's best friends with lipedema fat
My body has sentenced me
to a life of loneliness or
mediocre love
Take your pick
Go on, choose
There's not much time

Why do I hate my body so much?
Where does this self-loathing come from?
I'm the same body
I didn't change it like an outfit
So why does it feel different?
If I don't love it, nobody else will
Nobody else will love me
If I don't love me

(I know I'm sounding cliché)
But I have such loathing
I look at current photos of myself
& I think
How???
I never thought this way before
How did it get to this?
I don't understand
It wasn't my fault
I didn't ask for this
I didn't ask for the infection
& the lymphedema
I didn't ask for it
Yet every day, I punish myself for it
I punch my self-confidence in the guts
I punch it and punch it
until it believes my narrative
That I can't work the same
That no man will love me
Because of the change in my body
I've sentenced myself to
a life of pain
when it wasn't my fault

Do I judge people by their bodies?
Is that what this is about?
Have I looked at other people who
are overweight and thought
you need to get your shit together
& be healthy?
This is why this is happening
I can feel what it was like
to be on the other side
of my gaze

I've sentenced myself to
a life of being on the other side
of my gaze
I have to stop this
I have to stop this now
Is this how I would want my
daughter to treat her own body?
To subject herself to the impossible
beauty standards set up by patriarchy?
It's warped definition of what a normal body should be?
I am beautiful
I am beautiful
I am beautiful
I am beautiful
I will keep repeating this thought
I will keep saying it and saying it
until I am cured
of this self-loathing
of this self-hate
I do not need to hate myself anymore
just because some others dislike me
I do not need to stick to
the other side of their gaze
I do not need to feel it
I can allow their distaste for me
to run off me like water
I am beautiful
I am beautiful
I am beautiful
I am beautiful
I can do this
I can defeat this hatred
I can defeat this loathing
I will conquer

I will come out the other side a survivor
I will win
I will surpass
Because life is too short
I will dress to reflect this
and treat my body
the same way
I will throw away the old clothes I'm keeping
just in case I somehow fit into them one day
I will buy new clothes
I will never give up trying
I will go to my death bed trying
Because I don't want this anymore
I don't want to keep doing this
I have to nurture
and love
what's within

Hairs

When we stopped seeing each other
I grew out my hair,
underneath my arms, legs, everywhere
The last time I was that overgrown
I was unhappily married
But this time I was happy
In fact, I enjoyed showering
and studying my dark hairs,
around my cunt, on my thighs
I imagined you fucking me
all hairy, and it turned me on,
because I've never felt so strong
Maybe it was because you told me
you enjoyed fucking men,
and I felt like I was turning into one
in all the right ways,
becoming like you,
your surface barren of
unpredictable feminine emotion,
I wanted to be the man
you wanted to fuck

You don't like it? Don't fuck it

I tell you I've waxed my hairs,
that I'm as smooth as a baby's bottom
& you make a comment about my landing strip
say that it should make a departure like the rest of my hairs
But let me tell you something, Mr
Just 'cause you're the unofficial man
in my life, for the time being (lucky you)
don't give you the right to make calls like that
If you don't like it? Don't fuck it.
Because let me tell you something:
If I can't be bothered waxing
and my hairs grow out a bit, they grow
And if I feel like never waxing again, I won't
Why do you get the luxury of being all hairy
while I got to go through the agony of wax?
Nah, you don't like it? Don't fuck it
I really like you and everything
but I got to make this really clear:
(I know I'm exaggerating but this is a poem)
If I don't want to wear makeup, I won't
If I don't want to straighten my hair, I won't
If I don't want to dress up one day, I won't
You don't like it? Too bad
Whether I do or I don't
I still feel like a woman
Hairs or no hairs
If you see me as different
that's your problem
(not that you would, I'm just saying! xxx)
I know we're not even fucking anymore
but that's irrelevant
because we might or

we probably will
eventually
(maybe)

So let me say it again:

If you don't like the 'situation'? Don't fuck it.
You don't like it?
Don't fuck it.

Fuck off

Disclaimer: this isn't about you

Babe, I like you and everything
but I don't think you care about me
as much as I care about you
so I think maybe you should possibly

f off

Please don't be offended
I know you're a nice guy
and you *know* I'm a good person,
that I have a warm and open heart
But if you don't think
I'm the best thing since sliced bread

I think it'd be best for both of us if you please

fuck off

Being a single mum is fucking hard!
If you can't appreciate that,
see my bones breaking
underneath the pressure of it all
If you don't have the overwhelming urge
to be my dustpan and brush
I know this may seem abrupt
but please, fuck off

Even if I wasn't a single mum
If you don't adore me

I don't really see the point
I'm not interested in filling your holes
or you filling mine,
not interested in being anything for you
If you can't appreciate my person

I can't be bothered chasing anymore
I've got too much to do,
energy I'd rather expend elsewhere
Don't want to bang my head against a wall anymore
If you are not going to kick down my door to get to me

Fuck off

I'm a busy woman for fuck's sake
If you are not going to be there for me – FUCK OFF
If you're not going to cook for me – FUCK OFF
If you're not going to fix the kitchen cabinet for me –
FUCK OFF

Yes, I mean it

Fuck off
Fuck off
Fuck off
Fuck off
Fuck off

I really don't want to hurt your feelings
I've tried to tell you in so many ways
but you just seem to want to stay around me
I'm trying to be as polite as I possibly can
but you don't seem to understand
so I'm going to be really clear now

Please

I'm not joking

PLEASE, would you just please

FUCK OFF

Romantic

I psychotically love you
(2013)

It's insane I know
After all the abuse I've hurled at you
All your lying and cheating
But I can't fight it any longer:
I psychotically love you
And I have no idea if it's real love
All I know is I must be nuts
For feeling the way that I do
No man has affected me in this way
The words won't stop or go away
I saw your photo the other day
You are the most beautiful man
I have ever seen
The composure of you
To stand beside me, my muse
I have too much to say
I just can't make sense
Of it, or my feelings
Other than to submit
To what is woman

Because when I'm in your arms
The scent of you
Evaporates my existence
And I cease to
Kill us with my words
Student to teacher
You are my preacher
You eliminate my why
And I am at life's high

And all that I am certain of is
The warmth on your tongue
Should exist on my clit, always
You should push down my thighs
Persist while I resist
Licking it
Fast, fast, fast
Slowing, for eternity

And your hands and lips
Should push past and insist
On taking control of my breasts
Possessively
To pry my crossed arms apart
Because I never let any man
Touch them or lick my cunt
But with you I say
Do whatever
Open me, unwrap me
My pride is brushed aside
I may hide, behind my poems
Yell that I never want to see you again
But you know it's not true
I psychotically love you, babe
You bastard, arsehole, prick
And nothing does the trick
I can't erase you from my skin

All it would take is one look
The Antarctic glaciers that are your eyes
And my poems would shatter
Nothing else would matter
Except you and me

Even in my decision
To set myself free
I live with this love
That overfills my heart
Spills out onto my life
And drowns it

This is my reason
This is my truth
I psychotically love
YOU
(But I think I may
love myself more
hence our separation,
you dickhead!)

Asexual
(2015)

I am turned off males for life
and I am also not attracted to women
so I have come to the conclusion
I must be some type of asexual

Once in a blue moon
my female genitalia might bloom
but I just do my quick business
(although that's not even quick anymore
because nothing I can create in my mind
is intense enough to get my own rocks off)
and then I just get on with life

I don't know what to make of this
I do not aspire to become someone's mrs.
I don't even aspire to become someone's partner
I would find it an annoyance and a bother

It seems I have fucked myself over so many times
I have desensitised my hormones

Maybe I am a new spawn of species
mutated as a consequence of
excessive 21st century online dating
and overproduction of male bastard gene

A female-asexual hybrid
I am the newly spawned
Woman

Cypriot girl
(2012)

While I'm Cyprus, you ask me
if I can find you a nice Cypriot girl,
someone to love you, look after you,
clean the house and cook for you
But listen here, you dumbarse Cypriot wog
Why don't you fly over to Cyprus yourself
& find your own Cypriot girl
Why should I find a Cypriot girl for you
when there's one standing right in front of you
Only problem is she's not gonna clean your house
You can do it yourself
And she won't marry you either
But she'll cook for you (sometimes)
*Ate, pareta mas re koumpare**
Stop asking, find your own Cypriot girl
*Ge pareta mas***

Cypriot dialect, English characters. Quit it, mate
**Quit it*

Starfish 69
(2014)

If the words were whispered in your ear
you'd be here, in an instant

Starfish 69

You came over with your cheeky grin,
a bag full of your tricks
said 'I want to tie you up'
and I replied I can't come
without touching myself

'We'll see about that.'

Starfish 69
It was sublime, to say the least
I can't get it out of my mind
that Starfish 69

We've run out of time (again)
You ended it the other night (again)
But I can't forget, Starfish 69

Restrained to the bed
A limb tied at each side
Spread wide and ready for you
To do whatever you liked

It was the only time
I came in my life
Without the aid of my hand
I cannot understand how

You have this effect over me

It had less to do with the
way you licked me
more to do with your dick
fucking my face like that
I got so turned on
by it being in my mouth
I came all over yours

I think it has less to do with
the way that you lick me
more to do with how you trick me
time and time and time again
Restrained to your needs and desires
I am powerless to move, against you

And even if you decided to strip your dick
fuck me bare back while I protest and weep
hands and feet, trying to rip free
my body would arch and moan
as you filled me to the brim
with all that belongs inside me
(this is just a fantasy, not sure why,
wouldn't want it in reality xx)

My Starfish 69

You said I'm the best sex of your life
yet you still decided to walk away (again)
Life isn't fair, why does it have to end?
I've never come so hard in my life
Oh, Starfish 69, will I again taste your delight?
I've never felt so alive

With you by my side
I can take on the world

And what of you, my muse?
Strong enough to decline me now
Strong enough to cut me out now
You told me I'm your fantasy
that you touch yourself to me
almost nightly

Will we honestly succeed this time?
We always come back for more
Will we really be able to stay away?
Will we really be able to resist our play?
The to and fro, the push and pull of our game?

I'm curious to see how strong sexual love can be
Is it possible that our sex will always win in the end?
Or does the emotional connection with her score higher?
Do you underestimate the strength of our connection?
Or do I overestimate it?
And if our sex continuously wins,
maybe you'll have no choice but to submit
to letting me in, to your heart

Starfish 69

If the words were whispered in your ear
you'd be here, in an instant

Only time will tell me
how this will all turn out
But if I never see you again
always on my lips, always

the taste of our Starfish 69

Starfish 69
Starfish 69

Husbands
(2014)

Husbands.
Are only good for one thing.
Spent my life, searching for a husband,
just like all Greek girls are supposed to.
I found mine early
He was there for me
in all the ways a good husband
is meant to be there for you

But he didn't like me

Now I'm divorced.

I have spent four years alone,
searching for a partner
Men cross my path,
pile another brick on the wall

I keep imagining myself with a husband,
or a partner, and when I do
I get an awful feeling in my stomach
like I have been turned off the taste of men
vomited up too many times

But if I am turned off by men
And I am not attracted to women
What does that make me?
Asexual? A nun? One of a kind? An alien?

I am lonely

but I think if I were to live happily ever after
I would probably be unhappy

Fuck husbands
I'll be my own husband
I'll be the cute handy girl of my house

Free way
(2013)

They loop, the freeways
around the north, where I grew up
I like zooming down the stretch
music blablablaring doof doof
but I'm always stressing
because I get lost all the time
and then I start thinking
maybe I wasn't meant for freeways
must be more of a gridlock-kind-of girl

Back at home, on our way to school
my daughter asks me why we
sometimes go a different way
and I explain that it doesn't matter
which way you go because you
always end up where you need to be

I never slow down at speed humps
and one day, the round, blue glass icon
of Mary I have hanging around
my rearview mirror
that my mum gave me to bless my journeys
is going to eventually smash
against my front window
and God knows where
those shards are going to land
probably right in my eye

I needed something fixed the other day
so I called a repairer
He arrived in a white van

He tried but wasn't successful
He'd have to come back
with some new parts

I waited for him to come
but he never did
Maybe he got lost
or forgot my phone number
Then a strange thing happened
I was suddenly pregnant
So I got on the freeway
And I drove and I drove
I had no idea where I was going
My womb expanding
rapidly by the hour
I kept checking for the repairer
when a white van passed me
potentially I could have been
driving a few hundred metres
away from him but
on a completely
different piece of road
the way these
freeways loop

The contractions came on abruptly
So I pulled over the side of the road
And as day laboriously turned into pink haze
right there, I gave birth to Hope
That's when I realised
You never had my number
I was the one who contacted you
And you were probably waiting
All this time

Unable to move, bloodied and disorientated
I saw you zoom past on your motorbike
disappear into the sunset
Felt your fury in the wind
I held Hope in my hands
picked up my phone to call you
but your number was no longer valid

Cradling my baby, I cried
You're gone now
It doesn't matter
All fixed now

I carry Hope
Back on the free way
I don't know where I am going
It doesn't matter

Casual sex
(2015)

Men check to see what you are made of

early on in the situation

Go on a date
slide your true love intentions
across the table
& he'll stamp them
with his disclaimer

of

not interested in a
relationship right now

Give it up too soon
& they lose respect
for you

Make it harder & your value increases

Slip up and you probably
won't hear from them again

I used to worry about wrecking
my chances until I noticed

I was doing my own checks

He may think he is testing me

But the thing is —

I am testing *him*

If he flirts with me early on
yet doesn't have the goods to back it up
If he tries to get me into bed
I may let him but at the back of my mind
as we fuck and I come all over his perceptions
I am taking my marker and crossing him off

Because I am already thinking

He just wanted to fuck the poet

So it will never work out

He won't contact me again
& I'll hurl angry poems his way

And that's the end of the story

Fuck V Day
(2016)

My friend asks if
I want to go to a club
to dance to a UK DJ
on Valentine's Day
a possible step
towards getting
our love lives sorted

& I tell her
I always lock myself
indoors on V day
as I don't want to
subject myself to the
claustrophobia

I mean, why would I want to
saturate myself in couples
Hallmarking about the place,
hand-in-hand with conventions
Why would I consciously
put myself in a position
where I am on the outer,
the single freak show
and have couples
look down at me with
those poor pity looks

Fuck V Day, I tell her

When I think of V Day
I think of being nineteen

my first love sending me
little teddies from Cyprus,
throwing them in the bin
as I contemplated suicide
after we broke up
and how I have never
loved that way again

Do you know what I think?
Don't feel sorry for me, couples
I don't need a relationship
to validate my life
I don't buy into forever
I don't subscribe to white-picket fence
I'd rather take that bunch of flowers
& smash it on the memory
of my first love's grave

I'd like to take a bunch
for every fucking bastard
who fucked me over
and smash it over their head
(not that there have been many)

I would rather take those
love-heart chocolates
and stomp all over them,
get all those sentimental
bullshit Hallmark cards
and rip them into tiny little pieces
watch them fly in the wind
land on my first love's doorstep
I want to take all those Hollywood DVDs
put them in a bin and burn them

(except *My best friends wedding,*
Ten things I hate about you &
a few others I can't recall right now)

So no, I don't want to go out on V Day
Not one little bit

Red lipstick

You tell me you love kissing
red lipstick off my lips,
getting it all over your mouth,
so I make sure I always have it on

But sometimes you won't kiss it off
Like when we're on the couch
And I'm lying across you
And you're running your hand
Across my chest, up to my neck
And down again to caress my nipples
And I try to bring my lips to yours
And you say 'no, not yet'
And you keep me down
Those times is when I want you
To kiss the red lipstick off the most
So I close my eyes
Breathe heavily
Because your touch across my chest
Awakens every cell of my being
And with my eyes shut
And my underwear WET
I tell myself I have to be patient
And I lick my lips
Imagine what you taste like
While you touch me and watch
Taking pleasure in denying me

Until finally you lean down
Bring your lips down to meet mine
And have your way with them

Romantic

Why am I such a
Romantic when
It only gets me into
Trouble?

My boyfriend broke my heart at the dinner table

He broke my heart at the dinner table
because he didn't use the big dish
when he baked the corn chips
for the nachos

He used the smaller dish,
so there was no room to layer
with the chips then the cheese
then the chips and the cheese

& before he put the chips in,
he overcooked the mincemeat I had
pre-prepared earlier that week
and it got dry as fuck

When I tasted it
I was like 'What the fuck, dude'
He broke my heart
I couldn't take it
I burst into tears
Why couldn't he just use the bigger dish
like I told him to so many times?
Doesn't he have any respect for my food???

I love my boyfriend
(2019)

I love my boyfriend
but I want to date other men
Does that make me a slut
or a human?
Am I the woman
or the man?
I haven't kissed or fucked another guy
Because I'm scared
Don't want to crack
something that's so stable
Especially when I know
this relationship is so right for me
But there is a need inside me
for other dalliances,
that I'm not sure where they'll lead
My boyfriend says
everyone wants to fuck others
but he doesn't have a strong need
Not like me
Am I the woman or the man?
I don't know
All I know is I want to be me,
to date, explore, kiss, fuck, be,
wherever it goes, wherever it leads
I want no ties, no constrictions,
just like the Mediterranean Sea
Flowing, cool, salty, refreshing
I want to live
my life, my way
To have no man
say I can or can't say

Will we survive
if I am like this?
I don't know
He says he's okay
Releases me to my ways
& the future
is as unpredictable
as me

Poem for the lonely ones

This poem is for the lonely ones
This poem is for nobody else
It's a gift just for you
Don't worry, I'm lonely too
I know – it's hard, when you
don't have a special someone to hug
You may come from a broken home
Or you might not have found the
right one yet – don't fret
You are not alone. It's okay
I know it's not much
& who am I to you?
Your life may be coming apart
at the seams & even though
there are people all around you,
you may feel more alone than ever
It's okay. I understand.
I have walked the road of
alienation & loneliness and pain
Life is an endless path
I see it in my daughter's eyes
One day I won't be here
One day people will just remember me
Don't forget that once, on a lonely day
I sent you a hug through this poem
Maybe it made you feel less alone,
less lonely, for a minute
It's the perception that does it
In the end, we are all alone
All we have is ourselves
& moments,
precious moments,

like this one, right now
where you connect with me
through a poem
Take my hand. It's okay
I'm lonely too
I am lonely too

Man enough to cuddle me

Can someone please tell me
where I can find a man
strong enough to cuddle me?
To take me in his arms
during my insanity
explain that everything
is going to be okay

A man who understands
my tightly knit words
my raining hailstone words
are merely the amour
for the fragility and sensitivity
beating lonely in my heart

A man who will take all of me
along with my imperfections
into his arms, kiss my tears
and believe, despite all that I do
that deep down I am cute
and adorable

and I can sigh in relief right there
resting on his brave chest
knowing he too
is cute and adorable like me
strong enough
man enough
to cuddle a fierce
a whirlwind
a force of nature
woman like me

Who is she?

Hey, guy!

Hey, guy!
You, who thinks he's all that,
who sat at my dinner table
then called me a troublemaker behind my back
You, who everyone thinks is all that
The one who makes the girls swoon
and the guys sigh
Hey! You think you're a feminist
but you're actually a misogynist
Don't try and mansplain that you're not
You are!
You're selective with the women
you trample over aren't you?
Got to keep up those appearances
News flash!
The fact that you step at all is problematic
Hey guy – screw you!
You may be clever at disguising your stripes
But I'm on to you
You want to mansplain
why I shouldn't write this poem?
Try me

Greek men are inherently sexist (to their own kind)

Greek men are inherently sexist
(to their own kind)
I bet this is a problem
in other cultures too
They can't help it
They just are
It's subtle
Even in the feminist types
Either they expect us to do
their labour for them
so they can achieve
what we can't (because of our hurdles)
Or they think they're better than us
Like we can't possibly be as good
Because we are their servants
A Greek man is lorded and adored
as a pioneer, an original thinker
A Greek woman is cornered
A trouble maker
when she opens her mouth,
dares to offer an opinion
that might undermine her superior
Greek guys are inherently sexist
They can't help it
They just are
& if you are a man reading this
& you're annoyed by it
I'm sorry but you
probably are

Wog family gatherings

When you rock up to a
wog family gathering
and you're the only single mum,
it's never fun,
especially if you're pinning after a guy
who's not there

Some parts are okay,
like sliding into political
conversations with boys,
even though you know
it's not your place
and they give you
the slight side eye

I like to do chores at these gatherings.
Not because it's my patriarchal duty
(they can all go to hell)
I do the chores because it's
something to do to keep my
hands busy, keep me busy,
my brain busy,
so I'm not reminded of how
I never measured up
to their perfection

Hide in the shadows
Show only the bits of you
we can handle seeing,
so we can feel better about ourselves
& you can too

I'll hang on by a thread
and then, when I get in my car to leave,
I'll cry out all of my failures
to round myself off again

Mothers are supposed to be
(2019)

Mothers are supposed to be caring
Mothers are supposed to cook
Mothers are supposed to nurture
Mothers are supposed to clean
Mothers are supposed to pick up the kids
Mothers are supposed to protect
Mothers are supposed to comfort
Mothers are supposed to help kids with homework
Mothers are supposed to be proud
Mothers are supposed to put everything
    above their children
Mothers are supposed to put looking after
    their children above work
Mothers are supposed to be married
Mothers are supposed to be married to men who provide
    so they can achieve the above
Mothers are not supposed to leave their children for more
    than a few hours or a day
Mothers are supposed to work only if they have no choice
    other than to work
Mothers should only work the hours required
    to make ends meet
Mothers are not supposed to travel for work and leave
    their children in the care of others
Mothers are not supposed to pursue dreams if it means
    leaving their children in the care of others
Mothers are supposed to physically always be there
    for their children
Mothers are supposed to just be mothers
Mothers are supposed to sacrifice themselves
    for their children

Mothers are supposed to act like mothers
Mothers have responsibilities
Mothers who do not take on their responsibilities
    are selfish mothers
Mothers who don't act like mothers are bad mothers
Mothers who don't act like mothers are bad mothers
Mothers who do not act like mothers
    don't love their children
Mothers who have a break down because they can't cope
    with all the shit above, don't love their children
The world looks at women who are mothers through the
    judgmental lens of 'mother'
The world looks at women who are mothers,
    not as women, but as mothers
The world dictates what I can and can't do
    based on me being a mother
I am not acting responsibly unless I'm acting like a mother
I birthed a child and the world
    chains me to the word 'mother'
The world tells my child I am not a good mother
The world tells my child I am not a good mother
Other women tell my child I am not a good mother
This is what one deals with daily when they are a mother

Insanity sounds like
(2010)

Insanity sounds like
a three-year-old's wail
two hours into resisting naptime
fingers in mouth, pink cheeks
someone else's little girl, not mine

I join in, for the chorus

Insanity looks like
the single mother's pension
counting the coins for dinner
masturbating to possibilities
that will never come
insanity is like blocks in my head
black and white, shuffling
it's the words *I am a mother*
like cotton wool in my throat

You can turn to family in insanity
for communal mothering
turned manipulation
you can rely on everyone's
it was your choice
delivering a big *shut the fuck up*
to your one and only child
dropping her off to her dad's
for that moment of release

and repent

Instead, I wait on the highway

Insanity's arms are open wide
like trucks heading for heavens

I fling my arms

Breathe

Embrace

This is mothering
This is insanity

Mummy's gone away again
(2019)

Mummy's gone away again
to be someone else's hero
Mummy's gone away

Mummy said goodbye again
from the foreshore of the Danube
she said away
the aeroplane drifted
and you stopped your play, again
Mummy's gone away

Why can't I be more like what you need?
Why can't I stick
to that path
we were destined to be on
you and me?

Do I make a difference at all?
Or am I just abandoning my post
to pretend like I am?
A few people huddle around me
the money stays in their pockets
and where do I feed you, my love?
Where do I feed you?

Mummy's gone away again
Are you hungry for me, baby?
Mummy's away

Mummy loves you
But I am not enough

You deserve more than this
Mummy's gone

Ποια εν τούτη; (Who is she?)

Ποια εν τούτη;
Εν τζείνη, τζείνη η πελλή.
Τζείνη που αφήνει το κοπελλούι της τζαι γυρίζει.
Τζείνη η παλαβή. Η χαζή.
Τζείνη η αλήτισσα. Η πουτάνα.
Που κουβαλά τον παλιοφεμινισμό.
Τζείνη η αρνητική.
Ένεν η κοινωνία το πρόβλημα, αλλα τζείνη.
Τζείνη η πελλή.
Αν εσιωπούσε τζαι λίο;
Ούλον πάνω στην κελλέ μας.
Φεμινισμός, ρατσισμός, ούλα τα σκατά
Οι, εν την καλιώ πουθενά.
Εν διασκέδαση που θέλω, οι βάσανα.
Να πάει στο καλό
τζι αν θέλει να αλλάξει λίο
ξέρει τον αριθμό μου.

Who is she?
It's her, the crazy one
The one that leaves her child and roams the streets.
The dumb one, the stupid one.
The tramp, the slut.
The one that pushes stupid feminism.
The negative one.
Society is not the problem, she's the problem.
The crazy one.
If only she shut up a little.
Banging on our heads all the time.
Feminism, racism, all the shit stuff.
No, I won't invite her anywhere.
I want to have a good time, not have problems.

She can go on her merry way,
and if she wants to change a little
she has my phone number

My mummy yells like that because

My mummy doesn't talk loud because
she's trying to be annoying
My mummy doesn't talk loud to be funny
like all the wog comedy depicts
She doesn't shout and nag
for me to do things
in an over-the-top way
to be dramatic or indifferent,
my mummy yells like that
because she's been repressed
because she's been shut down,
my mummy yells like that
because she's trying to explode out
of the box patriarchy put her in to shut her up
My mummy doesn't yell to make some
wog guy comedy writer money
so they can keep getting the gigs
while us women sit on our seats,
my mummy yells because she was shipped off
to another country to be married
when she was nineteen
so she could pop out a couple of kids
and she had no choice in the matter
My mummy yells like that,
like a loud, aggressive whine
like someone is smashing bottles over your head
because she's fucking tired
she's fucking over it
she's over fucking knowing
that Haroula down the road
is still getting bashed by her husband 20 years later

and she can't say nothing but
'ti na kanoume?'
'what can we do?'
My mummy yells because she's over it
And she can't even say it
Because she doesn't know how
She's not even aware of it
And that's why it's my job
to write this poem
& to do something
about it

Smile
(for Grace Tame)

Don't cha really want to, babe?
You know you do
Come on, show us your teeth
You're so pretty, babe
Show it off, strut your stuff
Smile, come on, babe, come on
It'll really help us all feel better
Come on, seriously, stop
Stop making us feel uncomfortable
Stop being selfish
Women are meant to be beautiful,
vibrant, glow gracefully,
make small talk, stitch tapestry
They're not meant to be down
down in the dumps
They're supposed to smile
Smile, babe, do it, do it now
do it, do it, be professional,
be ladylike, or we'll punch
that smile into your face
do it, do it, stop fucking crying
smile, smile, see my hand?
see my hand? see it?
it's about to slap you,
you fucking bitch
just SMILE
SMILE!
that's it
that's better
SMILE

Grace Tame is an Australian activist and advocate for survivors of sexual violence. She was recently photographed with the Prime Minister of Australia not smiling and received much backlash.

I wish I was a cool Greek guy

I wish I was a cool Greek guy,
a cool Greek guy that everyone thought was really cool
The kind of cool Greek guy that everyone loves,
even the Aussies, and even my mum
A cool Greek guy that can say whatever he likes
and people still think he's really cool
even when he's talking a whole lot of fluff,
and uninspiring stuff
I'd get invited to all the really cool parties and events,
because everyone loves me and wants me around

I want to be a cool Greek guy who is always right
And he knows it
And everyone around him knows it
I'm not talking about the kind of Greek guy
who would find this poem funny
I'm talking about the kind of cool Greek guy
that would get into a huff about this poem
and be like 'hey, she's out of hand,
that chick need to be put in her place' kind of
    cool Greek guy

I'd rather be a cool Greek guy
than a shouty inappropriate Greek girl,
the kind that doesn't say what she's expected to say
doesn't act like she's supposed to act,
not only in the Greek community,
but to everyone, out there, in Australian society
and people think she's a *rezili*
I'm talking about the kind of shouty Greek girl
that doesn't take the hand of the cool Greek guy
and run off into the sunset with him

to make souvlaki, *baglava*, *koubes*,
or other Greek foods for the rest of her life
to offer them to the Aussies to win them over

I wish I was the kind of cool Greek guy that
from time to time got slightly intimidated by the
    shouty Greek girl
and had the power to put her in her place
in a very subtle way under the guise of care and coolness
But finally, I wish I was a cool Greek guy
who had never suffered any kind of repression
and instead had his sister making sandwiches for him
as he watched TV with his feet up

Migrant communities

We have the best street festivals,
in Melbourne they close off the streets
The souvlaki is amazing
OMG the pizza on Lygon Street
The default position of a Greek woman is
behind the kitchen sink
but who cares, man, who cares, man, who cares?

Opa! Greek culture is the best!
That Greek man who writes for the paper is so intelligent!
He has got so many important things to say!
But who is the whingy wog woman writer over there?
Who cares, man, who cares, man, who cares?

Did you go to so and so's wedding last weekend?
OMG, what an achievement, what a success
The men push us aside like we've got nothing
important to say,
always trying to put us back in our place
in the most degrading, offensive, patriarchal ways
But who cares, man, who cares, man, who cares?

Migrant communities around the world are big and wealthy
We have the film festivals
And music festivals
And writers festivals
With minimal female representation
The briefs have been met
People come to celebrate the façade of our culture
So who cares, man, who, cares, man who cares?

Migrant communities are governed and controlled by men
(sometimes good-Greek-girl feminists trying to get ahead)
And we want it to stay that way
Our cultures have rich histories to be celebrated
A great selection of Greek male fiction writers
So who cares, man, who, cares, man, who cares?

Have a *vasilobita*!
Who cares?
Have a souvlaki!
Who cares?
Have some pizza!
Who cares!
Have a Greek dance!
Who cares?
She's getting bashed
Who cares?
She can't leave her husband!
Who cares?
What will people think?
Who cares?
She's drugged up
to her fucking eyeballs
Who cares?
Let's take all this unpleasant shit
Shove it under the cultural carpet
And dance a *zeimbekiko* over it
Because who cares, man
Who cares, man, who cares?

To the Greek woman who came to see my show

To the Greek woman who came to see my show,
the one shrouded in repression

Dear, Greek woman

Darling, Greek woman

To the Greek woman who came and took my hand
after my performance while I was flurrying about
and forced me to stop into her eyes

To the woman who held my hand tight
and wouldn't let go until I paid attention

Dear Greek woman who said
thank you for saying all the things
we all want to say but can't say

as I nodded
and looked around at people
and was overwhelmed

To the woman
who grabbed my hand harder
& shook it until I had her
full attention
insisted I look her in the eyes
kita me sta matia
& repeated herself again
until everything around me ceased

and it was just me and her
looking into each other

To the woman who made me want to
pour all of my struggles into her eyes

To *this* beautiful image of Greek woman

I do it
so we can
both feel

normal

Cutting Through The Bullshit

When you are a woman like me

When you are woman like me
you have a lot of enemies,
when you are a woman like me

When you are a woman like me
people don't like you,
they exclude you,
they laugh about you,
they try to 'get you' but they don't,
when you are a woman like me

When you are a woman who is honest
people are infuriated by you,
when you tell it straight down the line
they want nothing to do with you,
they censor you,
they want you to go away,
turn a blind eye,
when you are a woman like me

Does freedom even exist?
We have been sold an expensive myth
Like soldiers at war
they want us to march
shouting their orders
they wonder why we bark
It isn't a male or female thing
It's the structures, it's their ways,
when you are a woman like me

But I'm done with charades
I won't sacrifice myself

just to play the stupid game
If they want to come for me let them come
I'd rather pay than play the game
With tears in my eyes
I'll stand strong and tall
and mightier than all of this
Because I am a woman like me
I will be a woman like me
No way they'll tear me down
I am a woman like me

Shit day
(2014)

Sometimes there are no words
to describe how shit you feel
Nothing nobody says can make it better
Stumbling through life
trying to find some meaning

realising there is none

Don't want to be uplifting today
just want to be sad and moody,
put on my computer programming hat
& take myself off to work

put some structure around my emotions

& it's not because I don't have
everything I want or need in my life
or that I am not appreciative

It's not that all

It's just that life is shit

My friend tells me to learn to meditate
& my sister tells me I'll be okay
& maybe I am in some kind of
post-traumatic stress phase
where the phase is
my whole fucking life

But that's the human condition, right?

I call Mum and tell her life's shit
& she tells me 'I told you so'
Finally I see what she sees, she says
& then we both laugh

Haha-haha-hahahhahahhAAA

I am trying so hard not to hate all men
but lately this is becoming difficult
It's not because all men are bad
as some of my very good friends are men
or because some man did something bad to me,
it's because of some deep-seeded reason
I haven't tapped into yet &
it will probably take my entire life
to tap into it and then I will die

It could have something to do with having to explain
that my art is not me, that I don't sit
with my legs spread waiting for a fuck
just because I wrote *Love and Fuck Poems*
Get in a car and travel ten thousand miles
from your point of perception,
that is where you will find me

Or maybe it's because lately
the thought of penises revolts me
or maybe it's that dream I had
that I was a polyamorous lesbian
or maybe it's coming to the realisation
that I don't think I am capable
of being in a relationship again

It could just be that all this is bullshit and I am just tired

and so with this knowledge I greet the day
my life, snapped into billions of pieces
thrown up in the air
and I am standing
amongst the rain
waiting to see
where all the pieces
will land
where I will end up
what I will be

I love my family

This poem has proven to be good therapy

I better get to work

Even when I'm dead

He'll hate me
even when I'm dead
I know he will
He has pushed me
to the ends of his heart,
to the parts that wilt away
at the edges
It doesn't matter that we're family,
or that I have tried
to make amends
There are people that it doesn't matter,
where you've bruised their ego
to the point where
even in death they'll carry
the bitterness

Friends who you block on Facebook

Friends who you block on Facebook
Friends who were once your friend
And by friends I don't mean
someone you see every now and then
I mean a real fucking friend
who holds your hand
when you're crying
& you hold theirs
when they're crying
and you buy them a red kettle
& two red tea mugs
reserved just for the two of you
& you laugh so hard you pee your pants

Those kinds of friends

The kind of friend where
it's like that for ten years

& then things change

But you weren't given any forewarning
that the rules had been re-written
& by the time you're drowning
in your tears
like stupid cliché
it's just too late

They're like a ghost in your life
But they're still alive
Because they've moved on

They don't have time
to discuss problems with you
They're a step ahead

They don't need you anymore

You're no one to them now
So you block them on Facebook
So they can't see any of your words
In case they're laughing
At how stupid you still are
And you want nothing to do with them
Because you don't recognise who they are
Not a speck of trust remains
So you try to move on
Block them on Facebook

I'm talking about those kinds of friends

Fake People

The thing is, they're everywhere
They're just not visible, not to the naked eye
The thing is, you don't know
Until it's too late, usually
Don't try to pull them up on it
Try and prove you care
Fake people are brilliant at being fake
Especially to themselves
You'll waste your breath
Just walk away
And don't worry, fake people
present themselves sooner or later
Because honesty always has a way
of slipping through the cracks
That's why it's honesty

Bitches who lie

I don't get bitches who lie
They start out acting like your best friend
Divert your hesitation
With unexpected gifts and kindness
Tell you it's never a good look to step on a woman
Gain your trust with their overwhelming understanding
And then, just as quickly as they came into your life
The Iron Gate snaps shut
And you're left wondering, did that even happen?
Then you start hearing whispers
A whisper here, a whisper there
Words you once spoke misconstrued,
their context removed
Whispers that spread like wildfire
Baffled, you reach out to ask *why*?
And it's a deafening silence on the other side

Didn't you once tell me you love me?

That's the thing, with bitches who lie
They're very good at padding their lies
With unexpected gifts and kindness
Start out like they're your best friend
So you never doubt for a second that they're lying
When they're bad mouthing others,
you never question them
Because *look how nice they are*
You never second guess them
Until things don't quite add up
And it's your name they're speaking
It's your name they're publicising
as the perpetrator

I'm sorry, bitch
but you're speaking lies
You're telling an unsubstantiated version of truth
so you can sleep better at night
Because you don't want to admit
you misread the whole thing
Side step accountability
Didn't you once tell me you love me?
Seems like love is just another whisper to you,
another juicy bit of gossip
That's the thing with bitches who lie
They need lies to survive
& the word 'friends'
is just really 'convenience'
& an audience
for their fiction

Bullies

Bullies seek out
vulnerable people with huge hearts
Like a vampire hunts blood
Take heed
Their behaviour is designed
so you think it's your fault
You're in a trance
Snap out of it
They're playing the victim
You're being bullied

Focus on the ones that love you
(2020)

Focus on the ones that love you
Focus hard
Do not let others enter your mind
Push them to the side
& allow your body to heal
Feel the acid in your stomach recede,
get drawn down your oesophagus until it dissipates
Let your body aches relax

You have put yourself through enough

Just because there's people out there trying to destroy
everything you've worked so hard to build
because you stand up for yourself and what you believe in
doesn't mean they have rights when it comes to what's in
 your mind

So push them away
Push them all away

You've spent enough years trying to please
narcissistic arseholes
How about *you*?
How about *you* for a change?
How about not that bitch trying to mow you down,
how about not that bastard trying to rationalise why it's
right that people exclude and punish you
for telling the truth
How about *no*!
How about you deserve more

How about you deserve better
How about you don't need to try and convince
 them anymore
How about stop apologising when you've already
 apologised!
How about you're not a trouble maker
How about people who always need to be right
 are upset that you're right
How about stop trying to understand *why* after you've sent
several olive branches when it wasn't even
your fucking fault!
How about there are actually people out there who enjoy
spreading lies and rumours
How about there are controlling arseholes
who get a kick out of it
How about you deserve better
How about you deserve more
How about bringing that energy back
Back to you. Where it belongs.
How about NO. How about NO MORE.
How about learn. Learn you can't reason with narcissists,
or people who show blatant disrespect and rudeness
and don't even apologise, or show remorse
How about NO
How about enough!
How about fuck them!
How about I'm not feeling bad anymore
How about I'm not making myself sick anymore
Or crying over people who don't give shit
How about I'm not feeling bad
for being who I am anymore
I'm bringing it back
Bringing all that energy back
Back to me

Where it belongs
To my body
Feels nice.
Focus on that
Close your eyes
Deep breath, all the way to your belly
Push them out
Then bring all the beautiful people in,
the wonderful, supportive people
Bring them into your mind
& smile
Don't feel bad
Smile

The disappearing

The disappearing of one's head up one's own backside
is an interesting phenomenon
Like how does one get to such a point where
they would even go to venture towards such a place?
I do believe it's a gradual process
Someone doesn't just magically disappear up there
It seems to be a systemic reinforcement
    of the self to the self
without much room for objectionable opinion

There are always signs of course,
that one is moving in such a direction,
like conversations not adding up
situations not being quite right,
like why are you badmouthing that person
and I'm not quite sure you're as great as you think you are,
and did you just throw me under that bus
and pretend like you didn't?
you know, things of that nature, etc, etc, etc.

The thing is, once one has poked themselves
into the region for a little look around,
and they like what they see,
all they need is a little positive reinforcement from others
who have also gone down such a path,
and then it's too late
They've disappeared. All the way up.
& really, at that point, there isn't much hope for them at all
Not unless they have a nervous breakdown,
get some much needed therapy
& come to the realisation

that they were not being very nice at all
Then they'll need to work hard to make amends
and begin the mammoth task
of pulling themselves out from under there

Cutting through the bullshit
(2015)

Last night, as I was watching *The Bachelor*
and analysing the reasons why
I am entertained by such stupid
degrading, misogynistic shows,
there was a guy on there
(one of the girls' guardians)
that was saying he always
tells people things straight up
ie cuts through the bullshit,
and I pondered for a minute
about how most of the time
(at least, like, 70% of the time)
people don't tell it like it is

Like the other week,
maybe instead of chucking a tanty
to one of my guy friends,
I should have just told him straight up
that I wanted to have sex with him,
because at least now
we'd still be on talking terms
rather than we probably
won't talk again.

I do that a lot, lose my shit when I'm
feeling impatient or vulnerable
Maybe I just need to be actually saying
what is really going for me
rather than being on
the attack all the time
like some, angry, angry, poet.

Don't get me wrong, you are definitely not right for me,
and maybe I like you, and you have done
some not nice things to me,
but yeah, that's what I wanted,
and I'm not sure how you would have reacted,
and you probably don't even deserve it,
but who gives a stuff anyway
because we'll probably never talk again
and anyway, this poem isn't about you, it's about me.

This is my life, and I'm tired of bullshit.
So I quit my computer programming job.
Because it was bullshit that I was doing it to begin with.
I did it because I felt like that's what I had to do,
and maybe it was also to please my parents a bit,
or make them happier that I was saving for a house
so I could have some security in my life.
What they don't realise is security is an illusion.
It's just a whole lot of bullshit
spread by the capitalist system.

Hopefully one day my parents will understand
that I am an artist, instead of trying to squeeze me back
into the conservative Greek box they've been
trying to squeeze me into my whole life
when it is clearly evident I don't fit!
Hopefully they will understand that my job is
to write poems like this that cut through
all the fucking bullshit out there
and join the chorus of all the other
writers who are trying to make
some kind of difference in this world

For example, why doesn't Tony Abbott
just admit he is incompetent when
Leigh Sales interviews him?
All the evidence points to the fact
that he clearly does not know
what he is doing,
but he still carries on
like we all can't see the bullshit

Hey, Tony: cut through the bullshit, man.
Don't you understand that your bullshit
is just perpetuating the problem of
all the bullshit shit people spin?
Don't you want to set a good example
as the leader of this sexist, racist country?
Shovelling money here,
shovelling it over there like it's snow
and you're some kind of little elf –
this isn't Christmas, Tony.
But if it is, you are not someone
I want coming down my chimney, that's for sure!
You put a pile of money into a thing called
the 'Book Council' for literature
and there's an article about it in *The Age*
but the whole article is full of spin and bullshit
and still nine months of newspaper articles later
we still don't know what the $9 mill Book Council is!

Sure, I'm embarrassed by this poem.
I thought about writing it and hiding it.
My parents want me to stop befriending
family on Facebook because
they are embarrassed
by what I write

& you know what:
I am embarrassed too.
I am ashamed to be a writer.
But that's all I know how to do
& maybe I've got some bullshit I need
to sort through so I can embrace
exactly who I am, cut through
find my truth, my reality
& work from there

Swallow the shit

Sometimes in life you got to
swallow the shit people throw your way
& be the bigger person
Sure, it tastes like hell
& you want to chuck it up
But you got to ask yourself:
is all the fighting and toing and froing
really worth your trouble?
Sometimes you just got to say
You're a fucking dickhead
(to yourself, in your head)
Put on a fake smile
Act submissive
Stereotypically female
Hand over the perception of control
& run all the way back to your life
Because you can't teach a dickhead
to be a good, decent person
That's why they're a dickhead

Love before politics

I will always choose
love before politics
I will respect your right
to say things I may not like to hear
because I love your humanity
& give you the space
to explore yourself,
without snatching the love
from under you

Always, when it comes to me
I put love before politics
because, politics cannot hold your hand
It cannot bring you hugs and chocolate
It is just a bunch of words
tied together into an idea
I will always try and understand
where you are coming from,
even If I don't agree,
because that's what you do
when you love someone

I always put love before
politics & trendiness &
cliques & the road to success
because at the end of that journey
there is only empty acceptance
Overflowing champagne glasses
Money
Fame rots
I will always choose love

With me, you know what you get
Integrity, honesty & love
That's what I will always choose

Don't say this, don't do that
(2014)

People are always telling to me
Why'd you say that?
Why'd you do that?
You can't say that!
You can't do that!
But why? Why the fuck not?
If I'm not breaking any law
Why can't I say this?
Why can't I do that?

When I was young
I was put in a box
and was told not to say say say
not to do do do
I was told shhhhhhhhh
I couldn't breathe in that box
I trembled, I shook, I went mad
in that box, that tiny box
much smaller than me

So I got married.

These days my parents are old
They can't even be bothered anymore
because they have learned the hard way
(because I am divorced)
that I'm going to say say say and
do do do what I want want want
See, thirty years of don't don't don't
is a long time of don't don't don't
So you can understand

when people say *don't*
it just makes me want to doooooooo

Why do men get respect when they say the same things
I say say say, but when I say them I don't don't don't?

and then I get labelled a hysterical woman!!!!!!!!!

AAAAAAAAAAAAAAAAAAAAAAAAAA!

Sometimes I get down down down
when people tell me I shouldn't have said this
or I should not have done that
But lately I been thinking
that it's too tiring keeping up with those people
because they remind me of that tiny box
and being in it all over again

See, I think people are too afraid to say say say
what they think think think or to do do do
what they want want want
And then they die die die

So I'm just gonna say say say
because I can't be any other way
and maybe it might help others
say say say and do do do

I say: say say say
and do do do
Don't care what people think
Just take it on the chin
SAY SAY SAY
before you're

dead dead dead

SAY! SAY! SAY!
Shout it! Shout! Shout!
SAY! SAY!
Do! Do!
SAY! SAY! SAY!
It's so cool cool cool
that I live in a country
where I can SAY SAY SAY
whatever I WANT WANT WANT
It's so liberating
It's so freeing

If you don't want to hear it
Fuck off! Unfriend me on Facebook!
Turn away! Walk away!
I don't care anymore
I'm done with it
I'm saying it
I'm saying what I want
I'm not listening
I don't care
Because it's just so awesome
It's so fucking awesome
Finally being

FREEEEEEEEEEEEEE

To be

ME

Credits

'A fucking arsehole-of-a-man killed his wife',
video created online, 2020.

'Are you a writer?', published in *Verge: Defiant*, by Monash University Publishing, 2023.

'Don't worry, I'll go', published in *Poetry & Place Anthology* by Close-Up Books, 2016

'Focus on the ones that love you',
video created online, 2020.

'In the name of justice, fairness, and victims of child sex abuse', video created online, 2020

'I wish I was a cool Greek guy', published in *Harana Poetry* (UK), 2021. Turned into a film starring Bruno Salsicce, 2022.

'Louie, Louie, Louie', video created online, 2017.

'Mediterranean madness', turned into a film, 2019. Finalist for the Multicultural Film Festival, 2022. Screened on SBS on-demand.

'Most of Melbourne is depressed', turned into a film, 2020, supported by Creative Victoria.

'My mummy yells like that because', published in *Verge: Defiant*, by Monash University Publishing, 2023.

'Oil-petrol-gas', published in *Avant-garde* (Cyprus), 2019.

'Pauline Hanson to chair a senate inquiry into the broken family law system', video created online, 2019.

'She's not normal', turned into a film, 2019.

'The literary judge', published in *The Paradise Anthology: The Music Issue* (4), edited by M. Crane, L. Charlton, 2011

'What are you wearing to the Melbourne cup?', video created online, 2019.

'Ποια εν τούτη; (Who is she?), published in *Bordertown III* by Transcollaborate, 2019. Turned into a film, 2019.

'Wog', published in *The Green Fuse* by Picaro Press, in collaboration with Varuna The Writers House and Byron Bay Writers Festival, 2010. Turned into a film in 2013 as part of the Good Greek Girl Film Project, supported by Australia Council (ArtStart).

—

Some of the poems in this book form the basis of Koraly's poetic theatre monologue, KORALY: 'I say the wrong things all the time', which premiered at La Mama in 2016, and other poems form part of her unproduced monologue which she developed with acclaimed director Stephen Nicolazzo as part of a Darebin Arts Speakeasy residency.

Acknowledgments

Thank you to all the people who previously published some of the poems contained in this collection. Thank you to my daughter for her cover design, editorial support, and for helping me with anything I ask for – you are the best daughter a mum could ask for. Thank you to David Cameron for editorial support and for always being there for me, and to Les Zigomanis for support, encouragement and friendship. Thank you to Christos Tsiolkas for the years of mentorship and for believing in me before anyone else did. Thank you to Ania Walwicz for your teachings that opened the door for my poetry and my art.

Some of these poems were written in Cyprus as part of my many tours of the island, so thank you to the Cypriot Ministry of Education for the funding support and believing in my art. Some were also written in the USA thanks to funding from the Cypriot government, and some in Poland as part of my UNESCO City residency in Krakow, so thank you also Krakow UNESCO. And to anyone else who I have forgotten, thank you.

About The Author

Koraly Dimitriadis is a Cypriot-Australian writer and performer who lives in Melbourne with her daughter. She has had poems published in Polish, Czech, Greek and Greek-Cypriot, and her short stories, essays and poems have been published in *Southerly, Etchings, Overland, Unusual Works, Social Alternatives, Meanjin,* S*olid Air* (UQP), *Resilience* (Ultimo/Mascara), *Foyer* (UK) and others.

Koraly's poetry films have been shortlisted for prizes, screened at festivals and have been televised. Koraly has performed internationally, including at The Poetry Café (London) and The Bowery (New York). Koraly's poetic theatre monologue "I say the wrong things all the time" premiered at La Mama. Koraly performed in Outer Urban Projects's Poetic License (Melbourne Writers Festival, 45 Downstairs, Darebin Arts).

Koraly's essays/opinion articles have been published widely across Australia, including international publications *The Independent* (UK), *Shondaland, The Guardian, The Washington Post, Al Jazeera* and *The Today show* (USA). Koraly is a professional member of the American Society of Journalists and Authors.
For her fiction manuscript, *We Never Said Goodbye,* Koraly was awarded residencies at UNESCO City of Literature (Krakow),

Wheeler Centre, Chantilly, HOANI (Cyprus), Me Meraki (Cyprus) and Moreland Council.

Koraly holds a diploma in professional writing/editing (RMIT) and a double degree in accounting/computing (Monash). She has spoken on panels, run workshops, taught poetry at RMIT, and has been interviewed on television and radio including ABC's "The Conversation Hour with Jon Faine".

www.koralydimitriadis.com

A fucking arsehole-of-a-man killed his wife	72
Aiia's poem	80
Are you a writer?	39
Asexual	109
Ashamed of my art	38
Being Brave	47
Bitches who lie	166
Bullies	168
Burnt bridges	41
Casual sex	120
Community TV choking	50
Cutting through the bullshit	174
Cypriot girl	110
Dear parking inspector who just gave me a ticket on Sydney Road	30
Deciphering the Arts Minister's speech	53
Don't say this, don't do that	181
Don't worry, I'll go	43
Dumb woman	14
Even when I'm dead	162
Fake People	165
Focus on the ones that love you	169
Free way	117
Friends who you block on Facebook	163
Fuck off	102
Fuck V Day	122
Greek men are inherently sexist (to their own kind)	135
Hairs	99
Hey guy!	134
Husbands	115
I am angry because	8
I can stay a bit longer, maybe	28
I don't want a gun	82
I love my boyfriend	128

I psychotically love you 106
I want to shoot Simon Armitage (poet laureate of England) . 35
I wish I was a cool Greek guy 150
I write my poems on the fly 33
In the name of justice, fairness, and victims of child sex abuse
 70
Insanity sounds like 140
Into the light 87
Like a political pawn 85
Louie, Louie, Louie 61
Love before politics 179
Man enough to cuddle me 132
Mediterranean madness 20
Melbourne's melody 22
Metro nightclub (The Palace) 27
Migrant communities 152
Missing in Brunswick (Part II) 74
Most of Melbourne is depressed 18
Mothers are supposed to be 138
Mummy's gone away again 142
My boyfriend broke my heart at the dinner table 127
My café residency kicked me out 45
My mummy yells like that because 146
Oil-petrol-gas 55
Part III: Death in Brunswick 77
Party 86
Pauline Hanson to chair a senate inquiry into the broken
    family law system 68
Poem for the lonely ones 130
Red lipstick 125
Romantic 126
She's crazy, she's nuts 91
She's not normal 2
Shit day 159

Smile	148
Starfish 69	111
Swallow the shit	178
Thank you, feminist Gillard	63
The box	11
The Cypriot rape case	58
The disappearing	172
The Free IUD	92
The great Australian dream	25
The literary judge	34
The work arsehole monster	17
The world	5
The world's interests	9
There is a dark part of me	88
Thin	95
To the Greek woman who came to see my show	154
What are you wearing to the Melbourne cup?	59
When you are a woman like me	157
White wog	37
Wog	36
Wog family gatherings	136
You don't like it? Don't fuck it	100
Ποια εν τούτη; (Who is she?)	144

www.ingramcontent.com/pod-product-compliance
Lightning Source LLC
Chambersburg PA
CBHW072002290426
44109CB00018B/2110